A PARENT'S GUIDE TO THE SCIENCE OF LEARNING

Supporting parents in the quest to help their children learn as effectively and efficiently as possible, *A Parent's Guide to The Science of Learning* translates 77 of the most important and influential studies on student learning into easily digestible overviews. This book will develop parents' understanding of crucial psychological research so that they can help their children improve how they think, feel and behave in school (and, indeed, in life).

Each study overview summarises the key findings from the research and offers tips, hints and strategies for how you can use them in your home. Covering important areas such as memory, motivation, thinking biases and parental attitudes, this book makes complicated research simple, accessible and practical.

From large- to small-scale studies, from the quirky to the iconic, this book breaks down key research to provide parents with the need-to-know facts. Essentially, it is a one-stop shop that offers guidance on how to parent even better.

A Parent's Guide to The Science of Learning answers the sort of questions that every parent wants to know but doesn't know where to find the answers. This includes the small, everyday questions through to the big, life-changing ones. Some of the questions answered in this book include:

- How much sleep does your child need?
- Should I actually help them with their homework?
- Why does my child forget what they have just learnt?
- How much screen time is too much?
- What can I do to help them do better at school?
- Is it really that important that we all eat meals together?
- How can I help my child learn to better manage their emotions?
- How can I encourage them to be a better independent learner?

A hugely accessible resource, this unique book will provide parents with the knowledge they need to best support their children's learning and development.

Edward Watson is the founder of InnerDrive, UK.

Bradley Busch is a chartered psychologist at InnerDrive, UK.

A PARENT'S GUIDE TO THE SCIENCE OF LEARNING

77 Studies That Every Parent Needs to Know

Edward Watson and Bradley Busch

Routledge
Taylor & Francis Group

LONDON AND NEW YORK

First published 2022
by Routledge
2 Park Square, Milton Park, Abingdon, Oxon OX14 4RN

and by Routledge
52 Vanderbilt Avenue, New York, NY 10017

Routledge is an imprint of the Taylor & Francis Group, an informa business

British Library Cataloguing-in-Publication Data
A catalogue record for this book is available from the British Library

Library of Congress Cataloging-in-Publication Data
Names: Watson, Edward, author. | Busch, Bradley, author.
Title: A parent's guide to the science of learning : 77 studies that every
    parent needs to know / Edward Watson, Bradley Busch.
Description: Abingdon, Oxon ; New York, NY : Routledge, 2022. |
    Includes bibliographical references.
Identifiers: LCCN 2021008258 | ISBN 9780367646585 (hardback) |
    ISBN 9780367646615 (paperback) | ISBN 9781003125709 (ebook)
Subjects: LCSH: Education–Parent participation. | Learning.
Classification: LCC LB1048.5 .W38 2022 | DDC 372.119/2–dc23
LC record available at https://lccn.loc.gov/2021008258

ISBN: 978-0-367-64658-5 (hbk)
ISBN: 978-0-367-64661-5 (pbk)
ISBN: 978-1-003-12570-9 (ebk)

Typeset in Interstate
by Apex CoVantage, LLC

ETW: To my parents who taught me so well and to my family Helen, Izzy, Ollie, Twiggy and Pavlov; thanks for putting up with my failings, for celebrating my successes and for being with me during the journey between the two.

BB: To my parents – thank you for your wisdom, patience and, above all, love that you have given me over the years. You have provided the best template to follow. If I can parent half as well as you did me, then he will be incredibly lucky. To my wife Pippa, I think you are a wizard at parenting, so thank you for letting me copy your magic.

From both of us, a big thank you to Routledge, our publishers, for continuing to take a chance on us. To our wonderfully talented graphics designer, Luis, a big thank you! We love your beautiful artwork – your creative talents are essential and much appreciated.

Thank you to the many researchers whose studies we have described. We hope that we have done your research the justice it deserves. And finally, thank you to all the members (past and present) of the InnerDrive team. In particular, thanks to DC, Blythe, Marayka, Emily, Izzy, Tom, Grace, Hattie, Ruhee, George, Lou and Matt. We have loved working with you all. A big thank you also to Dan – we couldn't have done any of this without you.

CONTENTS

About the authors   *xi*

Introduction   **1**

STUDIES   5

1   The one about memory   7

2   The one about aspirations and expectations   9

3   The one about the planning fallacy   11

4   The one about spacing your learning   13

5   The one about growth mindset   15

6   The one about predicting future behaviour   17

7   The one about teenagers and social rejection   19

8   The one about IQ and success   21

9   The one about parents and grades   23

10 The one about student resilience   25

11 The one about marshmallows and self-control   27

12 The one about mindset and purpose   29

13 The one about spacing and interleaving   31

14 The one about parents and failure   33

15 The one about revising to music   35

16 The one about the Dunning-Kruger Effect   37

17 The one about parental praise   39

18 **The one about effort being contagious**   **41**

19 The one about talent bias   43

20 **The one about retrieval practice**   **45**

21 The one about thought suppression   47

22 The one about self-analysis over time   49

23 **The one about asking "why?"**   **51**

24 The one about sleep   53

25 The one about mobile phones   55

26 The one about marshmallows, reliability and self-control   57

27 **The one about note-taking**   **59**

28 The one about Impostor Syndrome   61

29 **The one about reading out loud**   **63**

30 **The one about eating breakfast**   **65**

31 **The one about academic buoyancy**   **67**

32 The one about the Spotlight Effect   69

33 **The one about developing resilience**   **71**

34 **The one about phones and sleep**   **73**

35 **The one about pictures and words**   **75**

36 **The one about teaching others**   **77**

37 The one about experts overclaiming   79

38 The one about the IKEA Effect   81

39 The one about parental beliefs   83

40 **The one about motivation**   **85**

41 The one about student daydreaming   87

42 **The one about going for a walk**   **89**

43 The one about stress mindsets   91

44 The one about how to give better feedback   93

45 The one about self-talk   95

46 The one about parents and reading   97

47 The one about deadlines, procrastination and choice   99

48 The one about smart reputations   101

49 **The one about emotions and achievement**   **103**

50 The one about interacting with nature   105

51 The one about stress and uncertainty   107

52 The one about metacognition   109

53 **The one about picturing the process**   **111**

54 The one about parental warmth   113

55 **The one about how much we forget**   **115**

56 **The one about mindset, attitude and self-esteem**   **117**

57 The one about learning styles   119

58 The one about eating dinner together   121

59 **The one about electronic note-taking**   **123**

60 The one about the Bandwagon Effect   125

61 **The one about retrieval practice and stress**   **127**

62 The one about false confidence   129

63　The one about reading and background noise　　131

64　The one about transitioning to secondary school　　133

65　The one about drawing for learning　　135

66　The one about parental involvement　　137

67　The one about bad decision-making　　139

68　The one about age and self-concept　　141

69　The one about self-regulated learning　　143

70　The one about cognitive load　　145

71　The one about screen time　　147

72　The one about parents and sleep　　149

73　The one about summer learning loss　　151

74　The one about knowing the end is near　　153

75　The one about interleaving and discrimination learning　　155

76　The one about the Peak End Effect　　157

77　The one about the importance of failing　　159

TIPS　　161

1　Tips for improving memory　　162

2　Tips for improving mindset, motivation and resilience　　163

3　Tips for improving self-regulation and metacognition　　164

4　Tips for students　　165

5　Tips for parents　　166

6　Tips for overcoming thinking biases　　167

The studies　　*169*

ABOUT THE AUTHORS

Bradley Busch is a chartered psychologist. With extensive experience working in schools, he is a leading expert at helping schools utilise psychological research. Outside of education, Bradley works with elite athletes that include England international footballers and members of Team GB. He is the co-author of *Release Your Inner Drive*.

Edward Watson is a graduate of Oxford University who served seven years in the Army. After an MBA at The London Business School, he worked as a strategic management consultant for Marakon Associates before running businesses in the Computer Games Market. As well as working in the corporate, education and sport sectors, he is also the co-author of *Release Your Inner Drive*.

If you want to chat to Bradley or Edward about A Parent's Guide to The Science of Learning, *or about staff and student workshops, you can email them at info@innerdrive.co.uk.*

Introduction

The children now love luxury; they have bad manners, contempt for authority; they show disrespect for elders and love chatter in place of exercise. Children are now tyrants, not the servants of their households. They no longer rise when elders enter the room. They contradict their parents, chatter before company, gobble up dainties at the table, cross their legs, and tyrannize their teachers.

– Socrates

For thousands of years, parents have wrestled with the question of how to help their children achieve their full potential. It seems the frustration felt by Socrates is one that is still being felt today. Age-old questions such as 'how much sleep does my child need?', 'how do I help develop their motivation to do well at school?' and 'how can I help them improve their memory?' are just as pressing now as they ever were.

For better or worse, a big part of how we parent our children is heavily influenced by how our parents raised us. They provided a template for us to follow. But, unfortunately, many of today's parenting challenges have no historical roadmaps. Our parents didn't have to wrestle with questions like 'how much mobile phone use is too much?' and 'what impact does social media have?'.

As a result, this combination of unanswered old and new questions means that parenting arguably has never been more difficult and challenging. In the absence of historic guidance, where does one go to seek the answers? Can psychological research step in to fill the void?

The book you are holding seeks to provide some clarity and direction, as it is part of our quest to help children to learn more effectively and efficiently. And, most importantly, it will discuss how actually to bring about the desired change that we want to see in our children. We want to help the science of learning meet the art of parenting.

Even though there is a wealth of research on the science of learning, to date much of it has failed to get into the hands of the people who need it the most – parents.

There are three prominent reasons for this:

1   Most people aren't too sure where to look for this sort of research.
2   If you know where to look, you have to pay lots of money to read the journals.
3   If you get access to the studies, some of them are very hard to read and make sense of. For instance, this is how one of the results from a study we really like appears in its journal:

$$\text{Rating}(k) = \beta_1 \text{rating}^{(k-1)} + \sum_{i(k-1)}^{i(k)} \beta_2 \text{shocks}^{(k)} + \beta_3 \text{variable term}^{(k)}$$

In this book, we have attempted to solve these three problems. We have selected what we think are the 77 most important and influential studies on the topic of the science of learning, read them and then translated them into a simple-to-read and easy-to-digest format.

How we selected our studies

We have selected a range of studies from researchers at universities from around the world, from countries including England, America, China, New Zealand, Canada, Japan, Australia, Germany, Spain, France, Holland, Belgium and Israel.

Some of the studies we have chosen are iconic, some are quirky, some are large-scale and some have a small sample size. Some are very old, and some have been published recently. Some have tracked students for more than 40 years, whereas others were done in just one day. What do they all have in common? Every one of them seeks to help answer the question 'how can we help our students do better at school?'.

A word of caution

The Scottish poet Andrew Lange once said: "Some individuals use statistics as a drunk man uses lamp-posts - for support rather than for illumination". We think the same can be said for psychology research papers. Our understanding of how people learn is constantly developing - with new studies being released and some old studies failing to replicate. What we 'know' is not a fixed or static thing. Therefore, this book represents our current understanding based on psychological research.

One book can't provide a definitive answer. However, it can offer a bit of guidance. Each study is best thought of as one single thread, but if you take a step back, when taken together, they combine to form a rich tapestry that is *A Parent's Guide to The Science of Learning*. We hope this tapestry will provide a firm foundation for parenting our children.

How We Wrote This Book

This book isn't written like most other books. As well as writing about the findings of the science of learning, we have designed this book in a way that reflects them. So, for example, we have mixed up the order of topics as recommended in **Study #4** and combined pictures and words **(Study #35)**.

If you do want to read the studies on a particular area, then the topics that we cover are colour coded as follows:

Memory
Strategies to improve how much your child remembers things.

Mindset, Motivation and Resilience
How to develop their persistence, effort and attitude.

Self-Regulation and Metacognition
Helping your child to think clearly, helpfully and consistently.

Student Behaviours
The key student habits and processes that make a meaningful difference.

Parents
The fundamental choices, decisions and behaviours that parents make and how they impact their children's learning.

Thinking Biases
The faulty thinking habits and quirks that get in the way of learning taking place.

Studies

THE ONE ABOUT MEMORY

by @inner_drive | www.innerdrive.co.uk

THE STUDY

In 2013, researchers from Kent State University, Duke University, University of Wisconsin and University of Virginia published a review of hundreds of studies to explore which strategies are most likely to lead to long-term learning.

THE MAIN FINDINGS

1 Two techniques were rated as being very effective for improving long-term memory:

Retrieval practice: Students have to generate answers to questions. This includes past papers, multiple choice questions or doing practice essay answers.

Distributed practice: Sometimes referred to as "spacing"; doing little bits of work often instead of a lot all at once (i.e., cramming). Essentially, students remember more if they spread out their learning and revisit the same material across multiple sessions.

2 Two techniques were found to be fairly effective:

Elaborative interrogation: Asking yourself "why is this true?" or "why might this be the case?" This helps students think about the material and make connections with previously learnt information.

Interleaved practice: Interleaving is where students mix up the types of problems they answer, so as to avoid "blocking" their time on just one type of question.

3 Two techniques were found not to be very helpful:

Highlighting/Underlining: Despite being the *weapon of choice* for many students, highlighting material often fails to lead to long-term learning.

Re-reading: Although students may feel that they have learnt something if they can point to a whole chapter that they have read, this may not be as beneficial as they think.

Ref: Dunlosky et al, 2013, *Association for Psychological Science*

THE ONE ABOUT MEMORY

 ## RELATED RESEARCH

Numerous researchers from around the world have run studies that support these findings. For retrieval practice to be most effective, it has to be done at "low stakes", which means it does not increase stress levels of students and is not used as a form of judgement of their abilities. We still do not know the optimum time to space sessions for distributed practice, which is currently being explored.

There is evidence to suggest that many students actually prefer to use study strategies that are least likely to lead to better learning. For example, several studies (#20, #69) have found that, even though it leads to lower exam results, students were most likely to rate simply re-reading the core material as more helpful rather than other, more effective strategies, such as doing lots of quizzes and tests. Likewise, many continue to revise whilst listening to music, even though this does not help (#15).

PARENTING IMPLICATIONS

How can parents use these findings? It will vary depending both on the age of your child and the subject they are studying. The testing effect can be harnessed through regular short quizzes. Likewise, distributed practice is important in education systems in which students no longer do modular exams (such as in the UK), so encouraging your child to revisit previous topics throughout the year is even more important.

It is important that we teach our children what does and doesn't work. Each minute spent highlighting or re-reading is 60 seconds not spent doing something more effective. As the authors of this study state:

> A premium is placed on teaching students content and critical-thinking skills, whereas less time is spent teaching students to develop effective techniques and strategies to guide learning . . . teaching students to use these techniques would not take much time away from teaching content and would likely be most beneficial if the use of the techniques was consistently taught across multiple content areas, so that students could broadly experience their effects on learning and class grades.

THE ONE ABOUT ASPIRATIONS AND EXPECTATIONS

@inner_drive | www.innerdrive.co.uk

THE STUDY

Aspirations are not the same as expectations. The former is what you want to happen, whereas the latter is what you expect to happen. But how much impact does having high aspirations and expectations have on student performance? Does telling your child to reach for the stars make them more likely to do so?

Research from Bristol University tracked 770 students from over 640 schools to see if their aspirations and expectations had an effect on their GCSE results and if they went on to apply to University.

58%

THE MAIN FINDINGS

1 **Most students** (58%) have both high aspirations and expectations.

2 Students with **low aspirations and low expectations did the worst** at GCSEs, with those with **higher aspirations and expectations** getting, on average, **2 more GCSEs** graded A*-C.

3 Having **high aspirations and low expectations** often led to **low achievement**. These students were twice as likely to get less than 5 GCSEs at A*-C than their peers who had both high aspirations and expectations.

4 Students whose **parents expected them to go to University** when they were in Year 9 were **over five times more likely** to do so than the students whose parents did not.

Ref: Khattab, 2015, *British Educational Research Journal*

THE ONE ABOUT ASPIRATIONS AND EXPECTATIONS

 ## RELATED RESEARCH

Subsequent research has found that most aspiration interventions do little to improve a child's educational attainment. Having high aspirations but being unable to achieve them has been found to lead to student resentment, frustration and social withdrawal.

The research has been far more positive on the impact and predictive power of high expectations if combined with high aspirations. Students' high expectations of themselves have been found to increase their confidence that they will answer more questions correctly on a quiz. Research suggests that having high expectations is most beneficial if done at the start of the school year or at the beginning of a new project, as this allows students to approach the year or project with no negative pre-conceptions or ideas.

An interesting related area of research has focused on the impact that parental and teacher expectations have on student performance. In most cases, this has been found to help raise student performance. A word of caution, however: if expectations are too high and unrealistic, then this can lead to an increase in stress and anxiety (#43).

PARENTING IMPLICATIONS

Since this study suggests that combined high aspirations and expectations are important, it is interesting to consider how parents can help develop this. One possible way is to start by looking at our own attitude towards education, as evidence suggests that this may have a big impact on our children's educational achievement (#9).

These high expectations and positive attitude towards education can be conveyed through discussing how important school is, the overall value of education and how a positive attitude towards their teachers is important to learning and getting the most out of that education.

Another approach would be to help our children bridge the gap between aspirations and expectations. As the authors of the study note:

> [We] should encourage their students to raise and maintain high levels of aspirations. However, these high aspirations should be reinforced by equipping students, particularly those coming from poor and disadvantaged families, with necessary skills.

These skills include any that help harness the motivation that comes with having high aspirations that can be turned into better grades. These include strategies such as metacognition, self-regulation and effective memory strategies such as spacing (#4) and retrieval practice (#20) and teaching the material to someone else (#36).

THE ONE ABOUT THE PLANNING FALLACY

@inner_drive | www.innerdrive.co.uk

THE STUDY

The Planning Fallacy states that most people underestimate how long a task will take to complete. Keen to see if this applies to students, researchers asked pupils to predict how long various pieces of coursework and activities would take them to complete. They then measured how accurate the students were and under which conditions they were most likely to achieve their predictions.

THE MAIN FINDINGS

1 Over **70%** of students **finished their assignment later** than they had predicted they would, with the average time taken being over **55 days** compared to the average prediction of **34 days**.

2 Students **took longer to finish the activity than they predicted** regardless of the nature of the task, be it an academic piece of work, or everyday activity, such as cleaning their apartment or fixing their bike.

HOW LONG YOU THINK IT WILL TAKE

HOW LONG IT WILL TAKE

3 58% of students who spent time **actively recalling similar previous tasks** were accurate in predicting how long the next task would take.

Students **who did not use** this technique were only accurate **29%** of the time.

4 Students were more likely to **finish a task on time** if the deadline **was set for them**, rather than setting one themselves.

5 When making future predictions, students were **more likely to think about their future progress** instead of potential future obstacles.

Ref: Buehler, Griffin and Ross, 1994, *Journal of Personality and Social Psychology*

THE ONE ABOUT THE PLANNING FALLACY

 ## RELATED RESEARCH

A lot of research has addressed the importance of setting goals, deadlines and knowing how long is left in a task (#74). Setting goals can help students focus their attention, minimise distractions and enhance work ethic and persistence. Likewise, setting regular deadlines has been found to help students manage their time and energy over the course of the year as well as improving overall grades (#47). This is because the further away a deadline seems, the less impact it has on people's attention, which subsequently reduces how effectively they spread out their efforts.

Other research to help people better manage their time has revolved around minimising procrastination. One popular strategy includes just doing the task for a few minutes, since actually starting a new project is half the battle. Other techniques include improving self-regulation so that students are less likely to get distracted, as well as doing the hard and important tasks early in the day, as students probably have more energy in the morning than late at night.

PARENTING IMPLICATIONS

As students get older, independent study is emphasised more. Clearly, time management is an important skill needed for this, as is making accurate estimations on how long different tasks will take.

Results from this study suggest that there are two key things that parents can do to help children make more accurate predictions. The first is to break a task down and help them set short, regular deadlines. The second is to help them make clear, explicit comparisons to previous similar tasks they have done. Helping them draw similarities and distinguish differences, as well as reflecting on how long these tasks took, will help improve their planning time.

The researchers of this study offer a word of warning on this, though, noting that "it seems that people can know the past and yet still be doomed to repeat it". Parents can play a key role in helping their students learn from their previous mistakes. Indeed, the researchers state that "individuals will generate more realistic and accurate predictions if they take past completion times into account. This improvement in prediction should only occur, however, if participants' recollections are valid and if their present task is comparable with the projects that they recall". Parents are well placed to offer guidance and provide a sense of perspective on this.

THE ONE ABOUT SPACING YOUR LEARNING

@inner_drive | www.innerdrive.co.uk

THE STUDY

Researchers devised an experiment to explore the optimum amount of time to leave between revision sessions.

They had 1,354 students learn 32 obscure but true trivia facts. These included questions such as "who invented snow golf?" and "which European nation consumes the most spicy Mexican food?". They then divided the participants into 26 groups, each with a different gap before their next revision session and a different amount of time after that before their final test. They then compared how many successful answers the participants recorded in their final exam to see what was the optimum amount of time to leave between study sessions.

THE MAIN FINDINGS

✔ Spacing is more effective than cramming.

✔ The optimum gap to leave before you revisit the same material depends on how long you want to remember the material.

✔ The further away the test, the longer the gaps between study sessions should be.

The researchers found the following timings offer a good guideline:

y-axis: How Far Away The Test Is — 0, 50, 100, 150, 200, 250, 300, 350, 400

x-axis: Gap Between Revision Sessions — 0, 5 Days, 10 Days, 15 Days, 20 Days, 25 Days, 30 Days

3 Days · 8 Days · 12 Days · 27 Days

Ref: Cepeda et al, 2008, *Psychological Science*

THE ONE ABOUT SPACING YOUR LEARNING

 ## RELATED RESEARCH

The Spacing Effect is one of the longest and most enduring findings in cognitive psychology. It was first detailed in 1885 by German psychologist Hermann Ebbinghaus, who found that humans tend to forget large amounts of information if they only learn something once. This is partially why students suffer from a 'summer learning loss' over the school holidays (#73). Since Ebbinghaus, research has consistently shown the power of spacing out your learning (#55). This is an effective technique, as it allows time for the material to be forgotten and re-learnt. This process can help a student cement this knowledge into their long-term memory.

In some studies, using spacing instead of cramming has resulted in a 10-30% difference in final test results. This finding has been found in a range of tasks, including remembering key words, random facts or solving complex maths problems.

The gap between study sessions listed in this study offer a guideline only, as other research recommends slightly different gaps. The researchers of this study state: "to put it simply, if you want to know the optimal distribution of your study time, you need to decide how long you wish to remember something". As a rough rule of thumb, the closer you are to forgetting a piece of information (before it completely drops out of your brain), the more likely it is that you will benefit from revisiting it.

PARENTING IMPLICATIONS

The ability to retain and recall large pieces of information has become even more important for students. Parents can help students improve their long-term memory by helping them space out the material and revisiting it regularly. Just as actors don't leave all their rehearsals until the day before the opening night of a play, and athletes don't only train the day before the match, so students should regularly return to previously learnt material.

The authors of this study note that this is "at odds with many conventional educational practices – for example, study of a single topic being confined within a given week of a course". Committing something to memory takes time and repetition. Students must carefully consider this when making revision timetables, as it is not just the "what" that matters but the "when" as well.

THE ONE ABOUT GROWTH MINDSET

@inner_drive | www.innerdrive.co.uk

THE STUDY

Children ages 9-12 years old completed a problem-solving game and were then told that they had gotten 80% of the questions right. Some of them were praised for their natural intelligence, whereas others were praised for how hard they had worked. The researchers investigated how the students felt, thought and behaved in subsequent tasks.

THE MAIN FINDINGS

1 Children who had been praised for their **intelligence** were more likely to choose future tasks that they thought would make them **look smart**. Children who had been praised for their **effort** tended to choose tasks that would help them **learn new things**.

2 Children who had been praised for their intelligence said that they **enjoyed the task less,** when compared to the children who had been praised for their effort.

3 Children who had been praised for their intelligence were **less likely to persist on tasks** than the children who had been praised for their effort.

4 Children who had been praised for their intelligence **performed worse** in future tasks. The children who had been praised for their effort **performed better** in future tasks.

5 86% **of children** who had been praised for their intelligence asked for information about how their peers did on the same task. Only **23% of children** who had been praised for effort asked for this type of feedback, with the majority of them asking for feedback about what they could do better.

6 38% **of children** who had been praised for ability lied about the number of problems they solved in the task. Only **13% of the children** praised for effort did.

Ref: Mueller and Dweck, 1998, *The Journal of Personality and Social Psychology*

THE ONE ABOUT GROWTH MINDSET

RELATED RESEARCH

Since this study, many different researchers have studied the impact of having a growth mindset. Some, though certainly not all, have found that having a growth mindset leads to better grades. This effect seems especially true for students who have previously struggled with their studies. Away from exam results, research suggests that having a growth mindset has many other advantages. These include coping better with transitions (#56, #64), higher self-regulation, grit, positive social behaviour and using more effective revision techniques (#69).

Another fascinating area of growth mindset research is on the associated mental health benefits, with evidence suggesting those with a growth mindset are less aggressive, have higher self-esteem and have less depressive and anxious symptoms.

PARENTING IMPLICATIONS

This study highlights the complexities and importance of how we deliver feedback to our children. Too much praise can lead to narcissistic behaviour and create a culture of low expectation. The problem with praise such as "you are so clever" or "you must be so talented" is that it does not tell children what they need to do in the future in order to be successful. By praising their effort and/or the strategies they used, we give our children a template of behaviours that they can follow next time.

The authors of this study, from Columbia and Stanford University, comment that "children exposed to this intelligence feedback, with an emphasis on proving ability through high performance, were likely to respond negatively when they faced achievement setbacks . . . children given effort feedback, on the other hand, who valued learning over performance, were understandably less likely to fall apart when they experienced an isolated low performance".

Studies like this must make us consider the merit of calling certain students "gifted and talented", as it implies to them that it is their gifts and talents that will make them successful, not what they do with them (#8). Interestingly, evidence suggests this type of praise may also lead to an increased likelihood of students cheating to maintain this smart reputation (#48).

In the rush to embrace growth mindset, sometimes the message behind the research has been either diluted into "growth mindset is all about effort" or morphed into "anyone can do anything". Neither of these statements are accurate or helpful. Having a growth mindset is about the belief that someone can learn and improve.

THE ONE ABOUT PREDICTING FUTURE BEHAVIOUR

THE STUDY

@inner_drive | www.innerdrive.co.uk

Once a year, over four days in spring at Cornell University, students are encouraged to buy a daffodil. All the money raised goes to the charity the American Cancer Society. To help boost sales, access to daffodils is easy, as the campus is flooded with them, they do not cost much and students are made aware of the good cause that the proceeds will go to.

A month before the daffodils were due to go on sale, researchers asked 251 students if they were planning to buy a daffodil and, if so, how many they would purchase. Three days after the event, the same students were again surveyed in order to find out how many they actually bought.

THE MAIN FINDINGS

Before the daffodil drive

83% of students said that they would buy a daffodil. They pledged to buy an average of two daffodils. Interestingly, these students rated themselves as being more likely to buy a daffodil than their classmates.

After the daffodil drive

When the researchers questioned the whole cohort of pupils after the event, they found that only **43%** of the students had bought a daffodil.

Students also bought less daffodils than expected. The average purchase was 1.2 daffodils, as opposed to the two they had predicted.

Why are we bad at guessing our future behaviour?
Perhaps when predicting what will happen, we are more likely to think of ourselves and the situation with rose-tinted glasses. We are unlikely to accurately consider the obstacles and effort required. This means that students may have good intentions with their work, but may not always convert these good intentions into actions by themselves.

Ref: Epley and Dunning, 2000, *Journal of Personality and Social Psychology*

THE ONE ABOUT PREDICTING FUTURE BEHAVIOUR

 RELATED RESEARCH

Other research has confirmed that individuals are quite bad at predicting future behaviours, especially ones that will make us happier (#67). Evidence suggests that to make accurate predictions, we should take the average of a group. This is called "the wisdom of crowds". Surveying a group and taking the average helps to reduce self-serving biases and removes extreme outliers.

In terms of helping turn good intentions into action, creating a productive environment for behavioural change seems to be a powerful technique. This means minimising potential distractions for procrastination, increasing autonomy and tapping into intrinsic motivation by making things fun, mastering the task or creating a sense of purpose. These have all been found to help boost positive change.

PARENTING IMPLICATIONS

So if students are not very good at predicting their future behaviour, how can we best support students in their studies, especially when, as they get older, being an independent learner is more important? As well as taking future predictions with a pinch of salt, it is important to remember that these failed predictions are not necessarily caused by students lying - in this study, the pupils really did believe they would buy lots of daffodils.

Harnessing your child's energy whilst also planning what obstacles they may face and how they will overcome them seems key. It is not negative to talk about what may go wrong, as long as it is followed up with productive discussion about what to do in such an eventuality. This model of "if this, then I'll do that" is a subtle yet powerful strategy to help convert good intentions into actual behaviour.

THE ONE ABOUT TEENAGERS AND SOCIAL REJECTION

@inner_drive | www.innerdrive.co.uk

THE STUDY

Having to navigate the teenage years whilst learning and performing in school can be a real challenge for our children. Keen to test if they are less immune to social rejection than adults, researchers ran a fascinating study in 2010.

They had young teenagers, old teenagers and adults play an electronic game of catch. In a virtual online room, they were one of three players. Unbeknownst to them, the other two players were automatic bots playing to a set programme. To start with, the other two bots would include the participants by throwing the ball to them. Other times, they would exclude them, by only playing with each other. The researchers then compared how the participants thought and felt as a result.

THE MAIN FINDINGS

The researchers found that being socially rejected made all three groups feel worse. However, they also found that being excluded from their peer group had the following impact:

1 Both the younger and older teenagers felt **much worse** than the adults did.

2 Both younger and older teenagers had a **bigger drop in mood** than adults.

3 Younger teenagers had the **biggest increase in anxiety**.

4 Older teenagers had generally **lower self-esteem** than adults.

Ref: Sebastian et al, 2010, *Brain and Cognition*

THE ONE ABOUT TEENAGERS AND SOCIAL REJECTION

 ## RELATED RESEARCH

The authors of this study, from University College London and Purdue University, noted that their findings "suggest that teenagers are hypersensitive to rejection" and also stated that their findings "are in line with previous work showing that social anxiety is at its peak at age 15". This effect may be particularly pronounced in teenage girls, with one study finding that they suffer a significant decrease in self-esteem during their teenage years.

We now know more about the teenage brain than we ever did before. Its structure and function are different than an adult's brain. Other research has demonstrated how teenagers are more likely to take risks, need more sleep, struggle to read emotions and have less self-control than adults. Although we are all susceptible to peer pressure (#60), evidence suggests that teenagers are more likely to be influenced by the group and are more likely to make bad decisions when in the company of their friends than are adults.

PARENTING IMPLICATIONS

A person will never be surrounded by so many people their own age than when they are at school. If teenagers are more sensitive to social rejection than adults, then navigating their teenage years at school presents a tricky tightrope for them. Excessive levels of stress can hinder learning, concentration and memory, meaning that what happens out on the playground (and also online on social media after school) can impact what happens in the classroom. Therefore, it is important that we explicitly teach our children strategies that help them manage their anxieties and frustrations. This includes techniques such as self-talk (#45), deep breathing, refocusing and reframing.

It is also interesting to note the different reactions that teenagers and adults had in this study. This shows how two people can experience the same event and have very different reactions. This does not mean that teenagers are over-reacting when they experience social rejection. At this stage of their life, social standing is an important currency. It is crucial to find a balance between empathising with them whilst also putting the latest slight into perspective.

THE ONE ABOUT IQ AND SUCCESS

@inner_drive | www.innerdrive.co.uk

THE STUDY

How much of a child's success is down to their IQ? Do genes dictate success? And can you accurately predict which of your students are going to go on to be successful?

Dr. Lewis Terman was responsible for one of the largest ongoing longitudinal studies on gifted and talented students. Based at Stanford University in the 1920s, he initially believed that a person's IQ would determine their success. Their success both in school and subsequently in adult life were monitored (and still continue to be today).

The children in his study often affectionately referred to themselves as the "Termites". Dr. Terman believed that his termites would go on to be the leaders of their generation because of their genius-like IQ scores. The data is updated roughly every five years. As a result, we now know more than ever how important IQ is and what other factors determine success in both school and in life.

THE MAIN FINDINGS

As expected, the termite students went on to do very well at school. What is most interesting about this study is the results of the follow-up studies on these students.

After 25 years, Dr. Terman started comparing the type of career his termites had taken up. Some were doctors, lawyers and university professors. Others were filing clerks, policemen or fishermen. Surprised at the wide range, Terman famously commented that "we have seen that intellect and achievement are far from perfectly correlated".

35 years after his initial study, Dr. Terman compared the 100 most successful participants (referred to as As) with those who were struggling at age 40 (referred to as Cs). Researchers found that:

1

The As did indeed have a higher IQ than the Cs (157 versus 150), but researchers concluded that this was not very significant, as **small differences between high IQ** have little real-life impact.

2

One of the most important differences between the two groups was **their character traits**. From a young age, the Cs showed a lack of determination and persistence, whereas the As already showed greater "will power, perseverance and desire to excel".

Ref: Terman, 1925, *Genetic Studies of Genius*

THE ONE ABOUT IQ AND SUCCESS

RELATED RESEARCH

The Termite Study offers a fascinating insight into the predictive power of IQ. Other research has confirmed that a person's IQ has a large genetic component and is highly correlated with their academic performance, creativity, happiness, future earnings and even life expectancy. Clearly IQ does play a significant role in our lives.

Other research has highlighted the importance of mindset, resilience, emotional intelligence and grit in future success (#12). This has been associated with how well students cope with change, how they recover from setbacks and how they process feedback. Research has found that it is clearly not a case of nature versus nurture, but a combination of both. The important question is not "which has most impact?" but "which areas can we help improve?" and "how do we best do so?". Research on this is ongoing and is unlikely to ever reach a definitive answer.

PARENTING IMPLICATIONS

This study, along with others (#19), raises some interesting questions, namely: how good are we at predicting who is going to be successful? And how do we best nurture the skills that will help them to do well? Evidence suggests that in primary schools, high achievement is often due to date of birth: students born in the early months of the academic year have a massive advantage over their younger peers. What we think of as "talent" and "intelligence" in the early years may actually just be age-related.

Indeed, given the time spent worrying about predicted grades and future outcomes, it is worth considering if such worry really helps. On the plus side, it can be used to track progress and ensure that our children are getting the right level of support. However, it is worth considering the opportunity cost as each minute spent predicting the future is 60 seconds not spent helping students learn.

THE ONE ABOUT PARENTS AND GRADES

@inner_drive | www.innerdrive.co.uk

THE STUDY

It is one of the most common and important questions that parents ask teachers at Parents' Evening: "what can I do to best help support my child?" So researchers reviewed 37 studies on the effects of parental behaviours and attitudes on childrens' grades. This involved a sample of over 80,000 students and their families. They then made suggestions as to what does and doesn't work.

THE MAIN FINDINGS

Their study found that four of the best things a parent can do at primary and secondary school level to help their child's grades are:

1 Have high academic expectations

Having high aspirations and expectations of your child **has the biggest impact** on their grades. Parental expectations include how important school is, their attitude towards teachers and the value of education.

2 Regular communication

This includes developing and maintaining communication with children about their school life. This **helps parents nip any potential problems** in the bud before they manifest into bigger issues.

3 Good reading habits

This involves **reading frequently and regularly with your child**. This includes reading to them and encouraging them to read alongside you as well.

4 Homework rules

This revolves around having clear rules to deal with how they divide their homework and leisure time. Explaining why these rules are in place **can help them to make better decisions** regarding their independent study time later in their school career.

By contrast, researchers found that behaviours such as parental attendance of school activities and supervising homework did not make a significant impact on grades.

Ref: Castro et al, 2015, *Infant and Child Development*

THE ONE ABOUT PARENTS AND GRADES

 RELATED RESEARCH

A large body of research has confirmed the findings of this study; specifically, the power of high expectations and valuing education (#66). This impact has been found whether those expectations come from parents, teachers or the students themselves.

Likewise, developing good reading habits and reading for pleasure has also been associated with improvements in vocabulary, spelling, maths and general academic achievements. Given the importance of reading, it is worrying that in 2016 the National Literacy Trust reported that only 40% of teenagers enjoyed reading and only 24% said that reading was "cool".

This study's finding that it is important to have clear rules around homework time is an interesting one, as other research has found that students who do their homework themselves (i.e., without parental supervision) do better. This is because when students get older, their homework becomes more complex, and they need to take individual responsibility and ownership for their own success.

PARENTING IMPLICATIONS

The authors of the study note that "anyone concerned about education would like to know which malleable variables have the greatest effect on educational performance. But, unfortunately, it seems that the largest effects are associated with variables outside the scope of administrators or policy makers". This is good news for concerned parents, as the area that has the biggest impact is within their own control.

With this power comes great responsibility, but also great opportunity. It turns out that it does not require in-depth academic knowledge or large resources (i.e., money) to make a positive impact. Starting small and simple - such as regular conversations and setting clear boundaries - seems to offer a good launchpad for future success. Children often learn from what their parents do and not just from what they say, so it stands to reason that if we model the desired behaviour (i.e., good reading habits) they are more likely to replicate it themselves.

THE ONE ABOUT STUDENT RESILIENCE

@inner_drive | www.innerdrive.co.uk

THE STUDY

Calvin Coolidge, the 30th president of the United States of America, once noted that "nothing in this world can take the place of persistence. Talent will not; nothing is more common than unsuccessful men with talent. Genius will not; unrewarded genius is almost a proverb. Education will not; the world is full of educated derelicts. Persistence and determination alone are omnipotent". Whilst he might have been slightly over-exaggerating the importance of resilience, the desire to help students improve these skills is probably more popular now than ever. But is resilience something that can be learnt and developed?

Resilience, originally studied in young children suffering major traumatic events, has since been researched in both sport and business. A recent study has now turned the focus to resilience in education. Through interviews with students, researchers identified three key attributes that lead to resilient learners and suggested what academic institutions can do to help facilitate their development.

THE MAIN FINDINGS

Researchers found three key attributes behind resilience:

1 A sense of perspective

This included managing one's emotions, concentrating on things one can control and setting both short- and long-term goals. Central to maintaining a sense of perspective was the importance of self-reflection, which allowed students to manage new or uncomfortable situations.

2 Staying healthy

This helped students respond well under pressure and during adversity. Ways to do this included doing physical activity and participating in team sports, which prompted more social interactions. Identifying and celebrating successes and positive self-talk helped improve mental well-being.

3 Social support

The more someone isolates themselves, the more likely they are to brood over bad decisions. Maintaining good relationships with friends, family and teachers helps students either feel better about their setbacks and/or provides suggestions on how they can possibly overcome them.

Finally, the study looked at what academic institutions could do to help foster resilient environments for their students. They found that helping them experience and learn from failures in a safe environment and providing high-quality feedback that focuses on strategies and next steps, as well as access to extra-curricular activities, helped.

Ref: Holdsworth et al, 2017, *Studies in Higher Education*

THE ONE ABOUT STUDENT RESILIENCE

 RELATED RESEARCH

This study supports existing research that has found that resilience is something that can be developed by the individual as well as facilitated by their environment. A recent overview (#33) by leading resilience researchers highlighted that for an environment to facilitate resilience it needs to be both high in challenge and support. Too much challenge and no support results in excessive stress, burnout and isolation. Too much support but not enough challenge can lead to complacency and boredom.

Other strategies that have been found to help improve resilience include being open to new experiences, being optimistic, viewing decisions as active choices instead of sacrifices and focusing on developing one's skills instead of comparing oneself to others. Viewing setbacks as opportunities for learning as well as taking personal responsibility for one's own thoughts and feelings can help.

Research has also demonstrated that setbacks and struggling are not always a bad thing (#77). Those who have experienced some adversity tend to perform better under pressure in the future than those who have been wrapped in cotton wool. Experiencing failure has also been associated with higher levels of empathy, motivation and determination.

PARENTING IMPLICATIONS

The authors of this study note that "failure is a central part of learning, but its associated connotations need to be reconceptualised as a learning opportunity". Many children feel that:

mistakes = bad = avoid at all costs

Helping them understand that mistakes and setbacks at some stage are inevitable, and then providing them with strategies to capitalise on them, will help us develop resilient learners.

Taking time to talk with children about how to improve both their physical and mental well-being will help equip them with the energy and skills needed to navigate tough times. Likewise, teaching them skills such as self-reflection and how to set appropriate goals will benefit them.

#11

THE ONE ABOUT MARSHMALLOWS AND SELF-CONTROL

@inner_drive | www.innerdrive.co.uk

THE STUDY

If I offered you a marshmallow and told you that if you refrained from eating it for 15 minutes, I would give you two instead, would you be able to do it? In the early 1970s, researchers asked 92 3- to 5-year-olds this question. The original study and the follow-up studies 20 years later changed how we viewed self-control forever.

This study is important for parents to know. Firstly, it is so simple that you could easily replicate it yourself (and many have). Secondly, it is a longitudinal study, which means we get to track the path of the students in the study over many years. Third, and finally, it is one of the most famous studies in psychology and is a staple in most psychology and education handbooks.

THE MAIN FINDINGS

Some students, when given the choice between **eating a marshmallow straight away** or **waiting to get two marshmallows later**, could barely contain themselves and ate the first marshmallow straight away.

Other students were able to wait and delay their gratification, and as a result were able to get the sweet, sticky reward of the extra marshmallow.

Effective strategies employed by those who exercised better impulse control included distracting themselves from the temptation by thinking about other fun things, closing their eyes or sitting on their hands.

In **follow-up studies**, researchers found that the longer the students waited for their marshmallow as young children, the more likely they were as adults to be:

| More attentive | Socially competent | Academically successful | Verbally fluent | Able to deal with frustration and stress |

It would appear that the ability to delay gratification predicts individual differences in developmental outcomes. It would appear that "self-control is crucial for the successful pursuit of long-term goals. It is equally essential for developing the self-restraint and empathy needed to build caring and mutually supportive relationships".

Ref: Shoda et al, 1990, *Developmental Psychology*

THE ONE ABOUT MARSHMALLOWS AND SELF-CONTROL

 ## RELATED RESEARCH

Subsequent researchers have focused on what causes some children to seek instant gratification and why others are more willing to wait. Some researchers believe it is down to differences in the brain, with those who give in to temptation having less activity in their pre-frontal lobes (associated with conscious decision making and impulse control) and more in the ventral striatum (associated with addictive behaviours).

Other researchers think it may be associated with trust, with a different study finding that, if young children don't believe they are going to get a second marshmallow if they wait, they are more likely to eat the first one (#26). Finally, others have suggested that students who "fail" the marshmallow test may not do so because of limited self-control, but because they are acting very logically. If you grow up with very limited resources around you, it may make sense to take the immediate reward, as future opportunities to do so again may be scarce. A very recent study seemed to support this, noting that a child's background and environment is a better predictor of future outcomes than their ability to delay gratification on the marshmallow task.

PARENTING IMPLICATIONS

Is school one big marshmallow test? With an ever-increasing amount of distractions (including but not limited to mobile phones), the ability to improve self-control and delayed gratification has become crucial. Perhaps it is not surprising that recent research by the London School of Economics found that students who attended schools that have banned mobile phones get an increase in exam results. This, along with other studies (#25), may give parents room to reflect on when they allow their child to use their mobile phone.

Maturity can be described as the increasing gap between thinking something and deciding to act on it. As the brain develops during childhood years, significant developments take place that reduce sensation seeking whilst improving impulse control. As well as removing temptations, parents can help by having discussions about how to improve self-regulation and delayed gratification and why children should want to do so.

THE ONE ABOUT MINDSET AND PURPOSE

@inner_drive | www.innerdrive.co.uk

THE STUDY

This study explored the impact of teaching students how to develop a growth mindset (i.e., the belief that I can get better) and a sense of purpose (i.e., why I should care about what I'm doing). Researchers explored the impact of these interventions, if they were scalable, and for which type of student they were most beneficial.

This study was based on 1,594 students from 13 different high schools. Students were assigned to a control group, a group getting just a growth mindset intervention, a group getting a sense of purpose intervention or a group getting both a growth mindset and a sense of purpose intervention.

These interventions were designed to be brief and delivered online. The growth mindset intervention involved a single 45-minute online session that included information about how the brain develops and how students had potential to become more intelligent through study and practice, as well as having them summarise the key findings in a letter to another student. The sense of purpose intervention had students explain how doing well at school could help them achieve meaningful goals which included "making a positive impact in the world" or "making their family proud".

THE MAIN FINDINGS

1 Students who had a **growth mindset intervention** had an increase in their grades.

2 Students who had a **sense of purpose intervention** had an increase in their grades.

3 Students who had growth mindset and sense of purpose interventions were **more likely to complete** their courses in English, maths and science.

4 The above findings were most pronounced for students who had been identified as **struggling or at risk of dropping out** of school.

5 Both growth mindset and sense of purpose interventions **were found to be scalable**, meaning they could be delivered online to large groups of students.

Ref: Paunesku et al, 2015, *Psychological Science*

THE ONE ABOUT MINDSET AND PURPOSE

 ## RELATED RESEARCH

One fascinating study (#40) looked at creating a sense of purpose for students learning a new foreign language. Some were not given any reason for why they had to learn the material. Others were told they should try hard because it was what was expected of them, whereas others were told there would be a test at the end of the term. Finally, the last group were told the purpose behind it was that it would help their future career. The result? Those who had received the explanation of why learning this new language would be useful to them put in much more effort and were more engaged in the lesson.

Likewise, a range of studies have found that developing a growth mindset may be especially beneficial for struggling students or those who are at risk of dropping out. Some of these studies are worth noting, as their sample size is more than 100,000 students. Other benefits that have been associated with a growth mindset include coping better with transitions, persisting for longer, self-regulation, well-being, grit and feeling more in control of their lives.

PARENTING IMPLICATIONS

This study has clear implications for parents as it shows that both a growth mindset and a sense of purpose can be developed quickly and simply. A sense of purpose can be fostered by encouraging your children to reflect on how working hard and learning in school can help them to accomplish their future goals. This seems to be especially true if these goals involve other people or making the world better. A good starting point would be to have them complete the sentence: "doing well at school will help me achieve my goals because . . ."

Having high expectations that your child can achieve, improve and develop, along with helping them develop a range of strategies that they can call upon following a setback, will help. Finally, helping them understand that mistakes can be a useful learning curve and encouraging them to measure their success against their own high standards, instead of comparing themselves to others, will facilitate their mindset towards their education.

THE ONE ABOUT SPACING AND INTERLEAVING

@inner_drive | www.innerdrive.co.uk

THE STUDY

How much impact does the order and timing of questions that students answer have on how well they learn the material? Is spacing, which is doing little and often, better than cramming? Does interleaving, which is mixing up the type of problems, help more than blocking?

In the first study, researchers explored the difference between spacing out maths revision sessions over the course of a week, compared to doing them all in one sitting. In their second study they also measured the impact of working on the same sort of maths problems for the whole session against mixing up the type of questions the students had to answer.

THE MAIN FINDINGS

1 In the final test, students who **spaced out** their revision sessions got an average mark of 74%, whereas those who **crammed** their revision got 49%.

2 One week after their revision, students who interleaved the type of questions they answered got an average of **63%** whilst those that had answered the same sort of problem (i.e., blocking) got on average **20%**

Ref: Rohrer and Taylor, 2007, *Instructional Science*

THE ONE ABOUT SPACING AND INTERLEAVING

 ## RELATED RESEARCH

A lot of research highlights the benefit of spacing over cramming (#4). Essentially, doing one hour a day for eight days is better than doing eight hours in one day. Other studies have found that using spacing instead of cramming resulted in a 10-30% improvement in final test results.

A growing body of evidence also has found that interleaving the types of problems within a subject helps improve long-term retention, recall and performance (#1, #75). This is because this process gives students an opportunity to practice a range of strategies but also offers the chance to get better at identifying which strategy is most appropriate and likely to succeed. One such study that tested children throwing differently weighted bean bags at a target found that those who mixed up the order of the weights in their practice attempts performed better in the final test than those who practiced with the bean bags in ascending weight order.

PARENTING IMPLICATIONS

It is interesting to consider how most maths revision textbooks describe a problem (i.e., how to add fractions) and then give ten practice questions on that problem. Interleaving may take a bit more time than blocking. The students in this study did better on their mock tests straight after their study session; however, they did not learn it as deeply. This suggests that for long-term retention, parents should encourage their children to interleave their revision.

Indeed, the authors of this study note that the benefit of spacing is

> When practice problems relating to a given topic are spaced across multiple practice sets, a student who fails to understand a lesson (or fails to attend a lesson) will still be able to solve most of the problems within the following practice set, whereas a massed practice set ensures that this student will have little or no success.

Therefore, mixing up the type of problems they face and spacing this out over a large period of time will likely yield far better results. Encouraging your child to do this should make a significant difference.

THE ONE ABOUT PARENTS AND FAILURE

@inner_drive | www.innerdrive.co.uk

THE STUDY

After experiencing a failure, children often look to their parents to see how they react. But what impact does their response have on their child's mindset? Parents can view failure as either "enhancing" or "debilitating". An enhancing view of failure sees setbacks as a chance to learn and grow, whereas a debilitating view of failure sees setbacks as a source of shame and forms the basis of a negative judgement on the child's ability.

Researchers from Stanford University ran a series of studies with over 100 parent/child pairs in order to explore what impact parental mindsets and their view of failure had on the child's mindset. Their results offer guidance as to how parents can help young students develop a growth mindset (i.e., the belief that one can get better).

THE MAIN FINDINGS

1 Whether a parent had a fixed or a growth mindset **did not predict** their child's mindset.

2 Children **were very accurate** at assessing if their parents viewed failure as either potentially enhancing or debilitating.

3 Parents who **viewed failure as debilitating** were more likely to have a child with a fixed mindset.

4 Parents who **viewed failure as enhancing** were more likely to have a child with a growth mindset.

5 Out of all the parents, older ones were more likely to believe that failure could be **a helpful learning experience**.

As the authors of the study comment, "it may be that parents, like children, have mindsets that shape their own goals and behaviours, but that these beliefs are relevant to shaping children's beliefs only if they lead to practices that children pick up on".

They summarise by stating that "our findings indeed show that parents who believe failure is a debilitating experience have children who believe they cannot develop their intelligence . . . these parents react to their children's failures by focusing more on their children's ability or performance than on their learning".

Ref: Haimovitz and Dweck, 2016, *Psychological Science*

THE ONE ABOUT PARENTS AND FAILURE

 ## RELATED RESEARCH

This study is one of the few that directly examines how parental beliefs impact and influence their children's mindset. Most of the research to date has looked at how parental attitudes affect student performance (#66), with higher student grades resulting from parents who value education and have high but realistic expectations (#9). Other areas in which similar results have been found include attitude towards homework and positive reading habits. This study is even more pertinent when one considers other research showing the important role failure plays in how someone develops and improves over time (#77).

In terms of developing a growth mindset, other research has focused on parental behaviours instead of attitudes. For example, evidence (#17) suggests that the type of praise parents use when children are very young (1-3 years old) is a significant predictor of their child's mindset up to five years later. Other strategies to help develop a growth mindset include encouraging students to choose challenging tasks, encouraging helpful self-talk and focusing on developing skills instead of comparing yourself to others.

PARENTING IMPLICATIONS

The results from this study highlight how someone's mindset may not always be visible to others. It is internal and it is hard to accurately guess someone's beliefs. What is easier to see is their behaviour. This suggests it is not what parents think but what they do that matters. It is not their intentions but their actions that matter.

Any parents aiming to help their child develop a growth mindset should remember the importance of visibly dealing with setbacks, disappointments and mistakes in a positive way. The researchers conclude by saying:

> It may not be sufficient to teach parents a growth mindset and expect that they will naturally transmit it to their children. Instead, an intervention targeting parents' failure mindset could teach parents how failure can be beneficial, and how to react to their children's setbacks so as to maintain their children's motivation and learning.

This type of intervention not only could lead children to adopt a growth mindset but also could directly help improve their persistence and resilience by reframing their opinions on failure.

THE ONE ABOUT REVISING TO MUSIC

@inner_drive | www.innerdrive.co.uk

THE STUDY

Many students do their homework and revision whilst listening to music. Many of these students will swear that listening to their favourite songs helps them study. But does it actually help or hinder learning? And interestingly, does it matter what type of music they listen to whilst revising?

To answer these questions, researchers assigned students of a range of ages to one of four groups: the first revised in silence, the second revised whilst listening to music with lyrics they liked (which included songs from One Direction and Katy Perry), the third group revised to music with lyrics they did not like (which comprised of very heavy thrash metal bands), and the fourth group revised listening to music that did not have lyrics.

The participants then took a test on the passages they had been revising, rating how distracting their environment had been, as well as writing down their predictions for how well they thought they had done.

THE MAIN FINDINGS

1 Students who revised in **quiet environments performed over 60% better** in an exam than their peers who revised listening to music that had lyrics.

2 Students who revised whilst **listening to music without lyrics did better** than those who had revised to music with lyrics.

3 It made no difference if students revised listening to songs they **liked or didn't like**. Both led to **a reduction in their subsequent** test performance.

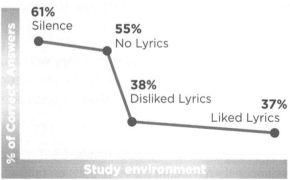

% of Correct Answers

- 61% Silence
- 55% No Lyrics
- 38% Disliked Lyrics
- 37% Liked Lyrics

Study environment

4 Students who revised **in silence rated their environment as less distracting** and accurately predicted that this would lead to better performances in subsequent tests.

Ref: Perham and Currie, 2014, *Applied Cognitive Psychology*

THE ONE ABOUT REVISING TO MUSIC

 ## RELATED RESEARCH

There are some known benefits to listening to music whilst performing certain tasks. It can be quite motivating, and it can improve mood (i.e., listening to a favourite song tends to make people smile). This is why many people listen to music in the gym. However, evidence suggests that it may not be great for learning; for instance, adding music to PowerPoint slides does not translate into better learning of new or complex material.

The misbelief that music aids learning may stem from a series of studies that have been dubbed The Mozart Effect. Participants in these studies appeared to be getting smarter and performed better in tests. However, further research has since revealed that this was not the case. Whilst listening to music before a task can make someone feel better, listening to it whilst trying to learn something new tends not to help. This is because music, especially music with lyrics, can take up processing space in the brain. This conflicts with the material you are trying to learn, effectively creating a bottleneck in your memory, since there is less space to process what you are revising.

The authors of this study, from Cardiff Metropolitan University, are in no doubt when they comment that "despite liking certain lyrical music, it is as detrimental to reading comprehension as listening to disliked music. Music without lyrics was shown to be less detrimental but, expectedly, performing reading comprehension was best in quiet conditions".

PARENTING IMPLICATIONS

It is important that we make it clear to our children the pitfalls of listening to music when studying. What is interesting to note is that this study found that students rated the quiet environment as less distracting and better for them, yet many students will continue to listen to music whilst doing their homework. Why would this be the case? Reasons could include doing so out of habit, confusing what improves their mood with what leads to good learning, alleviating boredom and thinking that everyone else is doing it.

Therefore, students need to know not just what they need to study but how they should study as well. There may well be a time and place to listen to music during the course of their studies, but not when they are learning new and complex material. As the old saying goes, "silence is golden".

THE ONE ABOUT THE DUNNING-KRUGER EFFECT

@inner_drive | www.innerdrive.co.uk

THE STUDY

In 1995, McArthur Wheeler robbed a bank in America in broad daylight. He was surprised later when he was arrested, as he incorrectly believed that covering his face in lemon juice would make him invisible to the CCTV cameras. Inspired by not only his incompetence, but also his lack of awareness, researchers Justin Kruger and David Dunning of Cornell University ran a series of studies to see if lack of ability is linked to low levels of self-awareness.

In their experiments they had participants perform various tasks and then estimate how well they did. The tasks included telling jokes, logical reasoning and grammar tests. Finally, researchers wanted to see what could be done to help someone more accurately assess their current ability levels.

THE MAIN FINDINGS

1 The **majority of people tend to over-estimate** their abilities. This finding is most pronounced in those with the lowest ability.

2 The level of **over-estimation decreases** the more able the participants is.

3 The Dunning-Kruger effect **has been found in a range of skills** that include logical reasoning, grammar and exam results.

4 The only group of people **who tend to under-estimate** their abilities are the most competent. This is often referred to as '**the burden of expertise**'.

5 Improving someone's metacognitive skills through training and workshops **was found to improve** the accuracy of their self-assessments.

Ref: Kruger and Dunning, 1999, *Journal of Personality and Social Psychology*

THE ONE ABOUT THE DUNNING-KRUGER EFFECT

 ## RELATED RESEARCH

This research appears to confirm what many notable figures from history have known. Socrates proclaimed that "I know one thing, I know nothing"; Charles Darwin noted that "ignorance more frequently begets confidence than does knowledge"; William Shakespeare in *As You Like It* wrote "the fool doth think he is wise, but the wise man knows himself to be a fool" and Thomas Jefferson once said "he who knows best knows how little he knows". Indeed, in *Star Wars* Luke Skywalker says that overconfidence by the dark side led to the Death Star being blown up.

Why do people not get better at recognising their incompetence, especially if they experience many failures? Research suggests that people may attribute their failures to external factors, such as luck or circumstance, as a way of protecting their self-esteem. This is not a bad short-term strategy to protect confidence, but unfortunately is found to be a poor strategy for long-term learning (#22), especially given how important failure is to one's development (#77).

PARENTING IMPLICATIONS

This study has three important parenting implications. Firstly, it is important to be wary of any-one who claims anything with 100% confidence (#37). Indeed, the authors of the study note that "the same incompetence that leads them to make wrong choices also deprives them of the savvy necessary to recognize incompetence, be it their own or anyone else's".

Secondly, it is important that students are aware of their current skill levels if they are going to improve them. If they have over-inflated views of their ability levels (#62), then it is less likely that they are going to reflect on how to improve and get better.

Third, and finally, we must find a good balance between helping our children understand their current level in a way that does not hinder their motivation. If they believe that their abilities are set and not going to change, then they are unlikely to put in additional work. Indeed, research suggests that students with this fixed mindset give up quicker, cope worse with transitions, have poorer coping skills and generally get lower grades.

THE ONE ABOUT PARENTAL PRAISE

THE STUDY

@inner_drive | www.innerdrive.co.uk

Researchers observed the interactions of 53 children aged 1–3 years old and their parents over a three-year period. During these interactions, the researchers recorded the amount of praise parents gave to their children and categorised it as either "process praise", "person praise" or "other". Process praise focused on the child's effort and strategies, such as "you must have tried really hard there" or "I really liked how you did that". Person praise was defined as praise that centred around a fixed positive quality, such as "you're so smart" or "good girl".

Several years later, when the children were 7–8 years old, the researchers returned to ask the students about their attitude to learning and what motivated them. They then compared the type of praise that the children had received years before to see if there was any correlation.

THE MAIN FINDINGS

1. 7- to 8-year-old children who had been praised for their processes, strategies and efforts when aged 1 to 3 were **more likely to have a growth mindset**, embrace challenge, value hard work and be able to generate strategies on how to improve.

2. The type of praise parents use is set **when their children are 14 months old** and remains consistent for the next two years.

3. Boys and girls both received similar amounts of overall praise; however, boys received far more process praise than girls did. **24.4% of praise for boys** was process-focused, whereas only **10.3% of praise that girls** received was for their processes. As a result, **boys were more likely** to have a growth mindset five years later.

4. The **mindset of a parent did not necessarily relate** to their child's mindset. What was most closely correlated was the type of praise the parents used. It was those interactions that most influenced their child's mindset.

Ref: Gunderson et al, 2013, *Child Development*

THE ONE ABOUT PARENTAL PRAISE

 RELATED RESEARCH

Several other studies suggest that praising a child for their effort and strategies is likely to help them develop a growth mindset and a belief that they can improve (#5). This is because new strategies can be learnt and acquired, thus promoting a more resilient mindset during adversity.

Other studies (#14) have examined the relationship between parental mindset and child's mindset. Researchers have found that how parents react to their child's setbacks has a significant impact. Parents who view their child's setbacks as an opportunity for their child to learn and improve, rather than as negative judgements on their child's ability, are more likely to develop a growth mindset in their children.

The finding in this study that boys receive more process praise and are thus more likely to have a growth mindset is an interesting one, as the results from other studies have been mixed. Some report no difference between boys and girls in terms of having a growth mindset, whereas other studies have found that girls are more likely to attribute failure to fixed factors rather than ones that they can change. Some research has also looked at subject-specific mindset and have found that the belief of a limited fixed ability in maths and science is more apparent in young girls than in young boys.

PARENTING IMPLICATIONS

The authors of this study, from The University of Chicago and Stanford University, note that "our findings are consistent with the idea that variation in parent praise can impact children's motivational frameworks and that the roots of this impact can be traced back to the toddler years". This would seem to suggest that reflecting on the type of praise we use with children at a young age can be very helpful.

The importance of parental praise is also interesting. Commenting on this, the authors also say: "given that children are likely to receive praise from many adults in their environment, it is remarkable that praise occurring during the thin slices of parent-child interactions [that they observed] provided insight into how children develop [a growth mindset]". Clearly the words children hear from their parents resonate with them long after they have been said.

THE ONE ABOUT EFFORT BEING CONTAGIOUS

@inner_drive | www.innerdrive.co.uk

THE STUDY

How do we get students to work a little bit harder? What impact does the person next to you have on how hard you work? And finally, if they are working hard, does that encourage you to do likewise?

Researchers had 38 students play a reaction-time game on a computer in pairs. Sometimes the tasks were on the same screen; sometimes they were on different screens next to each other. Some of the time they could see what their partner was doing, and sometimes they couldn't.

The researchers manipulated the game so that one of the pair had a more difficult task, which forced them to work harder. They then measured what impact this had on the other member of the pair.

THE MAIN FINDINGS

1 Students were **more likely to work harder** on a task if the person next to them was working hard.

2 It did not matter if a student couldn't see **what task the other person was working on**; if the other student was working hard, it still encouraged them to do so as well.

Why was this the case?
It may be due to the bandwagon effect, which is where people adopt the behaviours of those around them. Another reason may be due to our automatic need to imitate those around us (i.e., if someone next to you yawns, you are more likely to do the same). Another reason may be that as human beings, we are very aware of other people's thoughts about us and want to make a good impression.

Ref: Desender et al, 2016, *Psychonomic Bulletin & Review*

THE ONE ABOUT EFFORT BEING CONTAGIOUS

 ## RELATED RESEARCH

One of the first studies ever conducted in sport psychology, more than 100 years ago, found that people would cycle faster on a bike machine if they were being observed by others. Building on this, other research found that skills that were either simple or well learnt were performed better if done in front of others.

This is not all straightforward, however. A fascinating study found that each person added to a tug-of-war team resulted in each member putting in less effort. This is known as "social loafing" and often is caused by players believing that other people will compensate and pick up the slack.

It seems therefore that other people can help us work harder and improve our performance if a) they are also working hard and b) we know our own performance is being tracked.

PARENTING IMPLICATIONS

Other research has emerged that suggests that, when given the choice, people will choose environments that do not require them to put in high levels of effort. This suggests that the default setting for children when they are working independently may be one of preserving energy, not expending it.

This has some interesting implications for who students decide to do homework or revision with, since evidence suggests that working with someone who is working harder will encourage a student to raise their performance (#60). The friend that they like the most may not be the person who helps them work at their best. The authors of this study, from universities in Hamburg and Brussels, succinctly summarise their findings by stating that "simply performing a task next to a person who exerts a lot of effort in a task will help you do the same".

THE ONE ABOUT TALENT BIAS

@inner_drive | www.innerdrive.co.uk

THE STUDY

What are we more in awe of, natural ability or hard work? A lot of people in education and sport claim to really value the importance of persistence and resilience, but are we all secretly holding a "natural talent bias"?

Researchers ran a study where they played two pieces of music to a range of musicians. The first, they were told, was described as "a natural" who had early evidence of innate ability. The second was labelled as a "striver" as they had demonstrated high levels of motivation and determination.

In reality, both pieces of music were from the same professional musician. The participants in the study then had to rate which sounded better and which would go on to have a better career.

THE MAIN FINDINGS

1 Despite hearing music from the same musician, the participants in the study **rated the "natural"** as more talented, more likely to be successful and the better choice to join their orchestra **than the "striver"**.

2 At the start of the experiment, the participants had stated that hard work and training were essential for a musician to succeed. This view was endorsed more by the expert musicians. However, the expert musicians **were found to be more impressed** by the "natural" musician than their less experienced counterparts.

3 When given the choice of who they would like to hear play again, the **experts went for the "natural"** and rated their ability higher.

Ref: Tsay and Banaji, 2011, *Journal of Experimental Social Psychology*

THE ONE ABOUT TALENT BIAS

RELATED RESEARCH

A similar cognitive bias to the natural talent effect is the halo effect. This is when people are influenced by someone's initial positive performance when it comes time to assess their second piece of work. One such study found that teachers who graded a student's first piece assignment highly were more likely to give them a better grade on their second unrelated piece of work.

Research suggests that one way to avoid this is to anonymise the performer from their performance. Evidence suggests that having blind auditions in music and anonymous CVs for job applications helps to overcome this faulty thinking. It has been suggested that similar measures for student work may help mitigate this in schools.

PARENTING IMPLICATIONS

This study, from Harvard University, has interesting implications for how people view talent. As the authors of the study note, "almost as complex as talent itself is the ability to recognize it". If people are seduced by natural talent, then those who show early signs of higher ability may be singled out for increased or special attention. This is problematic, especially when you consider a recent piece of research showing that how well a child does at primary school is closely related to the month in which they are born. This means that children at primary school may appear more talented within a year group than they are, because of their relative age. This effect almost completely disappears by the time students leave high school.

Another issue raised by this study is how we subsequently help children develop their skills. If we say we value hard work and effort but our actions show our children that we actually value natural ability, then the latter message is more likely to be picked up. If children believe that hard work and effort will make little difference as they will always be behind their more "naturally talented" peers, then this may mean that they are less likely to put in hard work and demonstrate resilience?

THE ONE ABOUT RETRIEVAL PRACTICE

@inner_drive | www.innerdrive.co.uk

THE STUDY

Researchers studied the impact of different study strategies on how much students learn. One such strategy is retrieval practice, sometimes referred to as the Testing Effect, which describes the act of having to come up with an answer to a question.

They tested how effective this strategy was compared to simply reading and re-reading key passages. As well as comparing final test scores, they also measured how effective the students thought these strategies were and how interesting they found their revision sessions whilst doing them.

THE MAIN FINDINGS

1 If the final test was 2–7 days away, students who had **one study period followed by a session of retrieval practice did at least** **30%** **better** than those who had done two study periods of reading.

2 The longer you need to remember information, the **more powerful** the "Testing Effect" is.

3 The longer you need to remember information for, the **less effective** reading is.

Final Exam Performance

Proportion Final Recall

"Did it Help Me?"

Judgement of Learning

■ Reading, Reading, Reading, Reading   ■ Reading, Reading, Reading, Testing   ■ Reading, Testing, Testing, Testing

4 Students were most likely to rate re-reading as being **more effective** than retrieval practice. However, the students who used mainly retrieval practice **remembered over 50% more** than those who had just read and re-read during revision.

5 Students who had revised using retrieval practice found it **more interesting** than those who had just read the material.

Ref: Roediger and Karpicke, 2006, *Psychological Science*

THE ONE ABOUT RETRIEVAL PRACTICE

RELATED RESEARCH

The benefits of retrieval practice have been studied for more than a century and have been found to be especially strong during stressful situations, such as final exams (#61). Other research confirms that immediate feedback after testing can further enhance these benefits and helps students identify any potential gaps in their knowledge.

Other research suggests that replicating exam conditions whilst studying for a test further enhances students' ability to recall information in their final exam. Essentially, practicing the ability to recall information improves our ability to do so.

The findings from this study - that students incorrectly believe that re-reading is a better strategy than retrieval practice - is both interesting and alarming. However, if students are intent mainly on reading whilst studying, other evidence (#29) suggests they should do so out loud and with no background noise (#63).

PARENTING IMPLICATIONS

The results from this study, from Washington University, have important implications for how we can help our children learn key material in preparation for their exams. It suggests that students may be likely to choose ineffective strategies at the expense of more effective ones, unless we help educate them as to the best learning strategies.

The researchers also touch on another important bonus of using retrieval practice regularly when they state: "frequent testing leads students to space their study effort". This backs up existing research that shows that spacing out your learning leads to far greater retention and recall than massed learning (i.e., cramming). Therefore, it seems imperative that we teach students clearly not just about the importance of studying, but how to do so more efficiently and effectively.

The results from this study couldn't be clearer. Quizzes and tests don't just measure learning, they actually help accelerate it too.

THE ONE ABOUT THOUGHT SUPPRESSION

@inner_drive | www.innerdrive.co.uk

THE STUDY

In one of the most iconic studies in psychology, researchers asked participants to verbalise their thoughts for five minutes into a tape recorder.

They were told to not think about white bears. They were asked to ring the bell in front of them every time they thought of a white bear or said the words "white bear".

THE MAIN FINDINGS

1 Despite trying **not to think about white bears**, participants did so at least once per minute.

2 Participants were **most likely to think** about white bears when they reached the end of a sentence or in moments of silence.

3 Trying to not think about something makes someone **more likely to think** about that thing. This is known as **"The Rebound Effect"**. This is because people have a preoccupation with the thought they are trying to suppress.

4 Participants who were told to **focus on a red car** instead of trying to suppress thoughts of a white bear **fared better**.

They still struggled to not think of white bears, but **had less of a rebound effect** than those who simply thought "don't think of a white bear".

Ref: Wegner et al, 1987, *Journal of Personality and Social Psychology*

THE ONE ABOUT THOUGHT SUPPRESSION

 ## RELATED RESEARCH

The notion that people have unwanted thoughts that they want to stop dates back to Sigmund Freud's work in the late 19th century. Since then, further research has suggested that we have poor ability to disregard thoughts and information. For example, studies have shown that juries are influenced by information that the judge has told them to ignore. Likewise, other research suggests that people who try to suppress emotionally difficult events are more likely to suffer later in life from negative psychological and physiological consequences.

As well as the thought distraction technique used in this study, other studies have found that saying the word "stop" is effective at halting a train of thought. This has helped people manage frustration, overcome nerves, sleep better and stop dwelling on worst-case scenarios. People may not be able to control the first thing that pops into their head, but they can control subsequent thoughts and actions.

PARENTING IMPLICATIONS

Results from this study, from Trinity University and The University of Texas, show the difficulties – if not impossibilities – of trying to not think about things. As the authors note, "to suppress a thought requires that one a) plan to suppress thought and b) carry out that plan by suppressing all manifestations of the thought, including the original plan". Yet students often try this sort of strategy when it comes to preparing for pressurised moments, such as public speaking or exams. They may be influenced by their parents who, with good intentions, say things such as "don't rush", "don't mumble your words" or "don't misread the question". Thinking like this paradoxically makes those things more likely to occur.

This study concludes by stating that "suppression is difficult because thinking without focus is difficult". Indeed, attempted thought suppression often leads to a preoccupation with – and, indeed, rumination on – the thoughts one wants to avoid. This study suggests that it would be better to focus on what you do want children to achieve rather than on what you want them to avoid. This includes phrases such as "take your time", "speak clearly" and "read the question twice". The implication is clear: don't think "don't".

THE ONE ABOUT SELF-ANALYSIS OVER TIME

@inner_drive | www.innerdrive.co.uk

THE STUDY

Researchers examined if people downgrade their assessment of their past selves in order to inflate their feelings about their current achievements. Their study, entitled "From Chump to Champ: People's Appraisals of Their Earlier and Present Selves", makes for fascinating reading.

THE MAIN FINDINGS

1 Peoples' descriptions of their present selves were **more favourable** than their portrayals of their past selves.

2 This finding, of **criticising our past self** as a way of praising our current self, was **consistent amongst both students and adults**.

3 The **longer the gap** between their past self and current self, **the more likely** they were to criticise their past self.

4 Participants believed that their **current self was better** than their past self, even if no actual improvement had taken place.

5 People were likely to believe that they had **improved their personality traits**. However, this belief did not extend to their acquaintances, with participants more likely to state that other people had **remained the same**.

6 The **more important the skill was** to someone, the more likely they were **to believe** that they had improved it over time.

Ref: Wilson and Ross, 2001, *Journal of Personality and Social Psychology*

THE ONE ABOUT SELF-ANALYSIS OVER TIME

 RELATED RESEARCH

The results from this study support previous research which found that people are more likely to rate themselves as being happier now than they were in the past. Indeed, people have a very odd perception of time, with things that happened at either the start or at the end of an event weighing heavily on our minds (#76).

Other research suggests that the more motivated we are to feel good about ourselves, the more likely we are to praise our current self at the expense of our past self. This helps boost our current self-worth and insulates us from doubt, worry and nerves.

A wealth of research has found that most people rate their skills and personality as above average. Indeed, in Western cultures people are often encouraged to think highly of themselves. However, by criticising their past self, people can boost how they feel now without having to actually get better or confront the reality of remaining the same in the face of current evidence. This is similar to the Dunning–Kruger Effect, which states that having low ability often leads to an inflated sense of one's current ability (#16).

PARENTING IMPLICATIONS

Being able to accurately assess one's current level of ability is a fundamental part of learning. It provides the platform that all learning stems from. If your child believes they are progressing based only on an overly negative view of the past, then this can hinder their motivation to actually get better. As the authors of the study note, "by evaluating former identities less favourably than current ones, individuals can judge themselves to be improving".

They also go on to state that "just as advertisers creatively manipulate evidence to showcase constantly 'new and improved' products, so too might individuals repackage and revise themselves to highlight improvement on important dimensions". This may provide a short-term boost to children's confidence. But, unfortunately, this type of confidence is not very robust or durable. The best way to help children feel confident is to increase their competence through raising their knowledge and skills.

THE ONE ABOUT ASKING WHY?

@inner_drive | www.innerdrive.co.uk

THE STUDY

If we want students to remember key facts, should we a) simply tell them the information, b) tell them the information plus an explanation of why it is true or c) tell them the information and have them think about why this might be the case?

In order to answer this question researchers placed students in one of three groups. Some read a list of sentences, such as "The hungry man got in his car". Others read these sentences along with an explanation afterwards (i.e., "The hungry man got in his car to go to the restaurant"). Finally, the rest of the students read the sentences and then had to answer a question: "Why would he do that?".

THE MAIN FINDINGS

Students who had **just read the list of sentences** recalled, on average, **37%** of them correctly.

Those who had the **sentence and an explanation** recalled **35%** of them correctly.

However, those who had **seen the sentence** and had had to come up with **their own explanation** (i.e., asking **"why would he do that?"**) were able to recall an impressive **71%** of the sentences.

% of sentences correctly

80

SENTENCES	SENTENCES + EXPLANATION	SENTENCES + ASKING "WHY?"
37%	35%	71%

Ref: Pressley et al, 1987, *Journal of Experimental Psychology*

THE ONE ABOUT ASKING "WHY?"

 ## RELATED RESEARCH

A growing body of research has found that the more students must think and process information themselves, the more likely they are to remember it. This is why students who had to generate their own answers by asking themselves "why would that be the case?" outperformed those who had been given the explanation. Psychologists have labelled this technique "elaborative interrogation". A recent and very comprehensive review found that this is one of the most effective strategies students can utilise to boost their memory.

Additional research has examined other reasons why it is helpful to ask "why would this be the case?" or "why is this true for X but not for Y?". Possible explanations include that it arouses a sense of curiosity and that it helps link the new information to pre-existing knowledge. This, in turn, ingrains the new information into the long-term memory.

PARENTING IMPLICATIONS

This technique of asking yourself "why?" may be better suited to some children than others. For example, the authors of this study, from the University of Notre Dame, the University of Minnesota and the University of Western Ontario, note that "novices, lacking topical knowledge, often do not automatically link newly encountered relations to information that could make the significance of the relations more understandable and thus, make the material more memorable".

This suggests that elaborative interrogation may be particularly effective for students who already have a wide breadth and depth of knowledge, or as a final study technique once a lot of the learning has already occurred.

The benefit of this technique is that it means parents can help their children with their revision even if they aren't very knowledgeable about the topic. This is because we do not need to provide all the answers for our children when they are studying, but instead simply must ask them questions that prompt them to think deeper about the topic.

THE ONE ABOUT SLEEP

@inner_drive | www.innerdrive.co.uk

THE STUDY

We all do it. Only a few of us are getting enough of it and most of us want a bit more. On average we spend over 20 years of our life doing it, but the benefits of sleeping are still underappreciated. Despite The National Sleep Foundation recommending that teenagers need up to ten hours a night, many report getting less than seven.

Researchers reviewed the many different functions that sleep plays and how important it is in terms of students' memory, emotional regulation and mood. Their findings confirm that it is a fundamental part of the thinking and learning processes.

THE MAIN FINDINGS

1 Having **a good night's sleep** prior to learning allows students to create **new memory associations more effectively**. This is known as their ability to "encode information".

2 If students do not get **enough sleep**, it **hinders their ability** to commit what they have been taught to memory. This is known as an inability to "consolidate information".

3 When **sleep deprived**, people are more likely to forget positive memories. The opposite is true with negative memories, with tired students being more likely to retain and recall these.

4 **Excessive sleep loss** increases the likelihood of students displaying negative emotions, feeling stressed and being unable to manage their emotions.

Ref: Walker and van der Helm, 2009, *Psychological Bulletin*

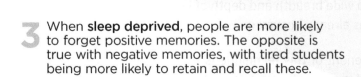

THE ONE ABOUT SLEEP

 ## RELATED RESEARCH

This review confirms the findings of other sleep research. Evidence suggests that, as well as being linked to memory, mood and emotional control, quality and quantity of sleep have a strong relationship to our ability to concentrate. This may be part of the reason that the amount of sleep students get has been found to correlate with the grades they achieve. But despite the importance of sleep, parents often don't know how much sleep their child is getting (#72).

Other research has found a link between getting a good night's sleep and our creativity and insightfulness, with participants twice as likely to find out the hidden rule to completing a puzzle if they had slept well the night before. Separate research has also found that teenagers who don't get enough sleep or who have irregular sleep patterns are more likely to fall ill, as sleep washes away toxins that have built up during the day.

PARENTING IMPLICATIONS

The need to educate students about the importance of sleep is paramount, as many may be unaware of just how important it is. The authors of this study, from the University of California, conclude their paper by stating "when troubled, get to bed, you'll feel better in the morning". It appears that, by doing so, children will also be more likely to recall what they have been taught previously and be more receptive to learning more in the future.

As well as teaching how important sleep is, we also need to teach our children about the common sleep mistakes. These include going to bed at different times each night (as this confuses the body's internal body clock) and taking excessively long naps earlier in the day. Other sleep mistakes include watching TV and using mobile phones right before bed.

Mobile phone usage late at night is particularly prevalent, with one study linking late-night texting or calling to declines in mood, self-esteem and coping ability. Evidence suggests that the teenage brain struggles with self-control more than the adult brain, meaning that teens may benefit from others (i.e., their parents) making that decision for them initially.

THE ONE ABOUT MOBILE PHONES

@inner_drive | www.innerdrive.co.uk

THE STUDY

Mobile phones are a part of everyday life. They have the power to connect people and can be great tools for learning. Most people have their mobile phone next to them for large parts of the day. But is there a darker side to mobile phones? Can the mere presence of a mobile phone negatively affect student performance?

To answer this question, researchers had students complete a concentration task with either a mobile phone or a notepad on the table near them. The students didn't use the phone during the experiment, it was just within their eye-line.

To gather further information, the researchers had students complete a range of questionnaires about themselves and also ran the experiment twice, once with someone else's phone near them and once with their own phone.

THE MAIN FINDINGS

1 The mere presence of a mobile phone led to a **20%** **reduction in attention, concentration and performance** in tasks that were demanding and complex (i.e., ones that students had to think hard about).

2 Students **performed worse** in these tasks, regardless of whether they could see their own **phone nearby** or someone else's.

3 This **reduction in performance was found to be true** regardless of the student's gender, age, how much they normally used their own phone or how attached they said they felt to it.

Ref: Thornton et al, 2014, *Social Psychology*

THE ONE ABOUT MOBILE PHONES

 ## RELATED RESEARCH

The numerous and wide-ranging costs of excessive mobile phone use have been well documented in psychological research. For example, research has linked students who are on their phone in class to worse grades, and those that use their phones excessively report higher levels of stress, anxiety and a fear of missing out. Frequency of students using their phone for social networking and texting is also negatively correlated to their grades.

A lot of research has been conducted on the impact of using a phone late at night, with people who do so for longer than 20 minutes at a time reporting less sleep each night and lower-quality sleep. Other research (#71) has also found a link between all screen time (i.e., phones, TV, tablets, computers) and a reduction in well-being, diet quality and concentration.

PARENTING IMPLICATIONS

A recent survey found that 81% of people report never turning their phone off. Therefore, having it on and nearby, even if it is not being used, is a common aspect of daily life. But at what cost? Students suffer from a drop in concentration when it is nearby, but as the authors of this study note, "the distracting effect of the cell phone's mere presence was not observed on the simple tasks, but was more apparent on complex tasks".

Why might this be the case? The authors of this study, from the University of Southern Maine, conclude their study by suggesting that "it is easier to maintain task attention when there are fewer stimuli present that may evoke thoughts unrelated to the task". Given that learning can be cognitively demanding, it is fair to assume that students should not be studying in sight of their phones. Out of sight really does seem to be out of mind.

Given this, perhaps it is wise for us to model this desired behaviour in front of our children, as if they always see the adults in their lives on their mobile phones, it is quite likely they will see this as the template for them to follow.

THE ONE ABOUT MARSHMALLOWS, RELIABILITY AND SELF-CONTROL

@inner_drive | www.innerdrive.co.uk

THE STUDY

The famous "Marshmallow Test" found that students who can delay gratification (i.e., work hard now on the promise of future rewards) do better at school and in life. In this test, researchers offered children one marshmallow. The children were told by the researcher that they could either eat it straight away or wait and be rewarded with two marshmallows later. The time the children held off eating the first marshmallow was used as a measure of delayed gratification.

But what if the students don't trust the adult giving them the instructions? Researchers divided students into two groups. Before giving them the choice of eating a marshmallow right away or waiting for another one, they had the students either see the adult break a promise (and therefore appear unreliable) or keep a promise (i.e., be seen to be reliable). They then measured how long the different students waited before they ate the first marshmallow.

THE MAIN FINDINGS

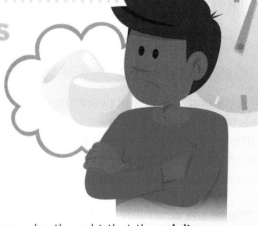

1 Children who thought the **adult was unreliable** waited for an average of around **3 minutes** before eating the marshmallow.

2 Children who thought that the **adult was reliable** waited for an average of over **12 minutes** before eating the marshmallow.

3 Out of **14 children** who had seen the adult previously be unreliable, **only one** of them was able to wait for the full **15 minutes**.

Out of **14 children** who had seen the adult previously keep their word, **nine** of them were able to wait the full **15 minutes**.

4 The impact of **seeing someone either lie or keep their word** impacted all students' ability to delay gratification. This was true regardless of age and gender.

Ref: Kidd et al, 2013, *Cognition*

THE ONE ABOUT MARSHMALLOWS, RELIABILITY AND SELF-CONTROL

 ## RELATED RESEARCH

This study advances our understanding of delayed gratification. Before this experiment, studies had predominantly put the emphasis on an individual's capacity to wait (#11). In fact, in studies that did not account for reliability as a factor, the average wait time before succumbing to the marshmallow temptation was around six minutes. This is half the wait time of the reliable teacher condition and twice as long as the unreliable condition in this experiment.

Other research has found that young children are particularly sensitive to uncertainty about their future. It therefore stands to reason that, if the children are not convinced that they will receive a later reward for delaying the gratification, then they see no reason to do so. As the authors of the study note, "waiting is only the rational choice if you believe that a second marshmallow is likely to actually appear after a reasonably short delay – and that the marshmallow is not at risk of being taken away".

PARENTING IMPLICATIONS

The authors of the study conclude by saying, "we demonstrated that children's sustained decisions to wait for a greater reward rather than quickly taking a lesser reward are strongly influenced by the reliability of the environment (in this case, the reliability of the researcher's verbal assurances)". If reliability is a significant mediator or children's ability to delay gratification, consideration must be given as to what we can do to help develop trust with our children and facilitate a consistent and stable environment, especially during times of change or uncertainty (#64).

Strategies include consistency and clarity. If children have a clear understanding of what is expected of them, what the rules are and what the consequences will be, then ambiguity and doubt will be reduced. Likewise, consistently and regularly enforcing these rules will help ensure reliability. They may not always agree with what you say, or always like what you do, but they will trust you more.

THE ONE ABOUT NOTE-TAKING

@inner_drive | www.innerdrive.co.uk

THE STUDY

Have you ever wondered if students should take notes during class or fully focus on what the teacher is saying? Does the previous experience of the learner with the material make a difference? Are some notes better for different types of learning than others? Research conducted at The University of California over 30 years ago has already comprehensively answered all these questions.

THE MAIN FINDINGS

Notes versus no notes

1 Students who **took notes** during a lesson performed **12% better** on a problem-solving test afterwards compared to those who took no notes at all.

2 However, students who **took no notes** did marginally better on questions that required them to recall **facts, stats and quotes** that were said.

The type of notes

3 In a follow-up study, students who **took summary notes** at either the end of the lecture or end of each topic did **10–15% better** on problem-solving questions and **13–17% better** on recalling facts than those who just took notes during the lesson.

Who benefits most from note-taking

4 Taking summary notes was found to benefit both students who were already familiar with the topic as well as those who were new to it.

Ref: Peper and Mayer, 1986, *Journal of Educational Psychology*

THE ONE ABOUT NOTE-TAKING

 ## RELATED RESEARCH

These results support a lot of the existing research on note-taking, with evidence suggesting that taking too many notes can be distracting and overload the working memory. This is perhaps why students who took summary notes instead of constant notes throughout the lesson performed better.

It is now commonplace for many students to take notes on their laptops, instead of using pen and paper. However, a recent study (#59) has found that students who used laptops were more likely to transcribe the lesson word for word without reflecting on it. Those who had taken notes with a pen and paper were more likely to write down key parts selectively and paraphrase them into their own words. This might play a key role in strengthening memories.

The other advantage of taking notes in one's own words is that it increases the chances of making an emotional connection to the content. Research has shown that the more emotionally powerful a memory is, the more likely it is to be stored in the long-term memory.

PARENTING IMPLICATIONS

Taking notes can be a double-edged sword. If done correctly, they can help your child pay attention during their lessons and block out distractions. They also give them a record of what has been said, which students can later refer back to. Additionally, as the researchers of the study point out, "note-taking can encourage the learner to actively build external connections between what is presented and what he or she already knows".

However, if done incorrectly, there can be a cost. Excessive note-taking can take up valuable processing time, which takes focus away from what the teacher is saying. This leaves students constantly playing catch-up. Writing down everything verbatim in real time does not leave enough time for students to think about, consider and relate what is being said to their existing knowledge and experiences.

It will help if we can encourage them to take some summary notes whilst emphasising the importance of fully listening to their teacher and reflecting on what they are saying. This combination offers the most sensible strategy for students.

THE ONE ABOUT IMPOSTOR SYNDROME

@inner_drive | www.innerdrive.co.uk

THE STUDY

Impostor Syndrome describes the belief that you are not as talented as others believe, that your success is down to luck and that one day soon your lack of ability is going to be exposed in front of everyone. Interestingly, it is often experienced by high-achieving individuals.

Initially, this was researched by a pair of psychologists who felt like frauds themselves. They wanted to explore the characteristics of Impostor Syndrome and what, if anything, can be done to help manage and overcome it.

THE MAIN FINDINGS

1 **Impostor Syndrome** was associated with:

Neuroticism
Increased fear and worry

Perfectionism
Unrealistic or unobtainable goals

Low self-efficacy
Doubt their abilities

2 People who suffer from Impostor Syndrome are **more likely** to rate themselves in a **consistently negative manner** across most situations.

3 20% of people were found to suffer from Impostor Syndrome, with it affecting **both men and women** pretty much equally.

4 **Social support** can play a high role in mitigating the effects of Impostor Syndrome.

Ref: Vergauwe et al, 2015, *Journal of Business and Psychology*

THE ONE ABOUT IMPOSTOR SYNDROME

RELATED RESEARCH

Impostor Syndrome has been found to be associated with depression and a decline in mental health. Interestingly, other research has found the prevalence of Impostor Syndrome to be even higher than reported in this study, with one journal reporting that 43% of students in the study had Impostor Syndrome tendencies.

It is interesting that this study found that both men and women equally experience Impostor Syndrome, because this contradicts previous research which had found it to be more common in females, with high-achieving women most likely to experience Impostor Syndrome. Indeed, a recent survey found that female students were less likely to describe themselves as "brave" compared with their male peers, with another study finding that young women feel less confident about entering the workplace.

Other research has focused on what developmental factors contribute to Impostor Syndrome. These have been found to include family conflict, perceived excessive parental control, an unhealthy and confusing message about the importance of high grades and a high fear of failure.

PARENTING IMPLICATIONS

So, what can parents do to help? The authors of the study state that "despite the accumulation of objective evidence suggesting the contrary, such as remarkable academic achievements and a successful career history, these persons are unable to internalize and accept successful experiences". The key, therefore, is to spend time helping our children identify what they did that contributed to their successes and help them to learn how to enjoy the fruits of their labour. Another strategy, as detailed in the study, is to ensure that they can identify and use the social support around them.

Constant feelings of being an impostor may result in students not putting themselves forward in situations that make them nervous, such as auditioning for the school play or trials for sports teams. Helping children to have the courage of their convictions and to step out of their comfort zones are life skills that will benefit them for many years to come.

THE ONE ABOUT READING OUT LOUD

@inner_drive | www.innerdrive.co.uk

THE STUDY

Dr. Seuss once commented that "the more that you read, the more things you will know. The more that you learn, the more places you'll go". But is there a way to read better that means that you are more likely to remember things?

Researchers ran a study where they had students study a list of words in four different ways. These were reading out loud, reading in silence, hearing a recording of themselves and hearing a recording of someone else say the words.

THE MAIN FINDINGS

1 The researchers found that the study conditions that were most effective through to least effective were:

▶ **Studying by reading the words out loud**

▶ **Studying by hearing a recording of yourself**

▶ **Studying by hearing someone else speak to you**

▶ **Studying by reading in silence**

2 The gap between reading aloud and hearing a recording of themselves was quite small, with only **3%** difference in the final exam separating them.

3 The biggest gap was between the studying by reading the words out loud and reading them in silence, with the former performing **12%** better than the latter.

Ref: Forrin and MacLeod, 2018, *Memory*

THE ONE ABOUT READING OUT LOUD

 ## RELATED RESEARCH

The increase in learning caused by reading out loud is an example of the Production Effect. The Production Effect is caused by producing something with the new information right away in order to anchor it in your mind, rather than it drifting away because of other distractions. This is why drawing whilst learning helps, as it produces a new picture (#65).

Reading out loud initiates the Production Effect by utilising a combination of three processes: it is an active event (i.e., you are not passive during it), it requires an element of visual processing (i.e., seeing the words) and is self-referential (i.e., "*I* said it").

These results also confirm previous findings from research (#57) that suggest that when students learn information using a combination and variety of senses it leads to an increase in learning. This is because a multi-pronged approach provides a range of connections in the student's brain, ensuring that the material is more likely to be ingrained in the long-term memory (#35).

PARENTING IMPLICATIONS

We all want to encourage our children to be good readers. And since many students often choose and prefer to read their notes as part of their revision, the results from this study are very important for parents to know, as they show that some methods of revising by reading are better than others. Teaching our children about the importance of reading out loud instead of in silence could help aid their learning and performance in exams.

The authors conclude by stating that studying and rehearsal "is so valuable in learning and remembering [as] we do it ourselves and we do it in our own voices. When it comes time to recover the information, we can use this distinctive component to help us to remember".

However, a word of caution is needed. Although reading aloud was found to be the most effective of the options available in this study, other research has shown that simply reading the material is a lot less effective than other strategies, such as retrieval practice (#1, #20). Therefore, only relying on reading one's notes during study sessions, even if this is done aloud, may not be the most effective way to learn the material.

THE ONE ABOUT EATING BREAKFAST

@inner_drive | www.innerdrive.co.uk

THE STUDY

Many students report skipping eating breakfast on a regular basis. But is there a cost to this?

To find out, researchers ran a study that compared students who ate breakfast, drank a glucose drink instead, or skipped breakfast altogether. As well as administering concentration tests throughout the morning, the researchers also ran a memory recall exam and had the students report how they were feeling.

THE MAIN FINDINGS

Concentration levels

1. All students had **a dip in their ability to focus** as the morning went on. However, if students had **eaten breakfast,** this decline was **reduced by 50–65%** compared to those who hadn't.

2. For the first few hours, **having a glucose drink** instead of skipping breakfast actually led to a **bigger drop** in students' attention levels.

Memory recall

3. In a memory test conducted four hours after a revision session, students who had **not had breakfast** suffered a **12%** reduction in their score. Students who had **only had a glucose drink** for breakfast had a **27%** decline, with those who **had breakfast improving** their performance by **3–5%**.

Alertness

4. Students who ate breakfast felt the **most alert over the course of the morning**. A glucose drink gave an initial boost for the first few hours before dropping to the same low levels by mid-day as those who had missed breakfast.

Ref: Wesnes et al, 2003, *Appetite*

THE ONE ABOUT EATING BREAKFAST

 ## RELATED RESEARCH

As well as the benefits to memory and attention demonstrated in this study, a wealth of research addresses the far-reaching benefits of eating breakfast. For example, eating breakfast has been linked to better eating habits throughout the day and improvement to both physical and mental health, as well as boosting energy levels.

Authors of a different study found that "individuals who consumed a cereal breakfast each day were less depressed, less emotionally distressed and had lower levels of perceived stress than those who did not eat breakfast each day". Why might this be the case? Authors of a different review found that "missing meals, especially breakfast, leads to low blood sugar and this causes low mood, irritability and fatigue". It seems that missing breakfast isn't just associated with poorer mental health, it actually causes it. Similar results have also been found for students who skip eating dinner with their parents (#58).

Finally, eating breakfast is associated with better physical activity. In a separate study on school students, both boys and girls who sometimes ate breakfast were found to do less physical activity than those who always ate breakfast. This is one of the reasons why those who skip breakfast are more likely to become obese and have higher levels of cholesterol.

PARENTING IMPLICATIONS

Educating children about the importance of eating breakfast is key. Left to their own devices, many will be tempted to miss it or have to a glucose drink substitute. Doing so can have serious consequences for their academic performance. For example, a different study found that the odds of an 11-year-old achieving an above-average score on a test were twice as high for those who ate breakfast as for those who did not.

The authors of the study couldn't be clearer when they say: "this study provides clear evidence that cereal breakfast has a positive effect on the cognitive function of school children, particularly towards the end of the morning". In the quest to best help one's children, it turns out that one of the simplest - ensuring they eat breakfast - may be one of the most powerful.

THE ONE ABOUT ACADEMIC BUOYANCY

@inner_drive | www.innerdrive.co.uk

THE STUDY

One of the least known psychological concepts in the area of mindset and motivation is that of academic buoyancy. Whereas resilience tends to refer to a person's ability to overcome large stressful events, academic buoyancy instead focuses on a student's ability to overcome the everyday challenges of school. These challenges include things like doing poorly on a piece of homework or working under the pressure of coursework deadline. As such, it is an important area within educational psychology.

Researchers explored the key components of academic buoyancy and how it can be developed. Their results make for essential reading for those interested in helping students flourish whilst at school.

THE MAIN FINDINGS

The researchers conclude that there are **five components of academic buoyancy** that can be targeted to help students overcome the everyday challenges they face at school.

They labelled these components as "The Five Cs"

Confidence
The self-belief that students have that if they work hard then they will have the abilities needed to successfully complete a specific task.

Co-ordination
Better planning, preparation and time management to avoid procrastination.

Commitment
Displaying high levels of resilience, determination and persistence.

Composure
The ability to manage nerves, anxieties and stress.

Control
Focusing on what is important and what they can control.

They also found that **"The Five Cs"** of academic buoyancy **apply to both male and female students**, as well as **younger and older pupils**.

Ref: Martin et al, 2010, *British Journal of Educational Psychology*

THE ONE ABOUT ACADEMIC BUOYANCY

 ## RELATED RESEARCH

Research on academic buoyancy is still in its relative infancy. There is cause to be optimistic, with many of its associated components - such as self-regulation, growth mindset and metacognition - associated with a range of positive outcomes (#52). Resilience, although similar but still distinct from academic buoyancy, has been more heavily researched. Ways to develop resilience include ensuring high levels of challenge and support, helpful self-talk and attributing successes to internal factors (#10, #33).

Another interesting area of related research has found that female students score significantly higher on anxiety scales and report more academic hassles. In terms of age, evidence suggests that the early teenage years are a particularly challenging time with regards to both fluctuating motivation and emotional control.

PARENTING IMPLICATIONS

Within their research paper, the authors of the study offer a clear and succinct breakdown of how parents could apply these findings to their children. They write:

> Developing self-efficacy (confidence) can involve restructuring learning so as to maximise opportunities for success, individualising tasks where possible, addressing and enhancing students' negative beliefs about themselves and developing skills in effective goal setting. Work into self-regulation and goal-setting also provide direction for enhancing students' planning (co-ordination) and persistence (commitment).

With regards to goal-setting, encouraging students to set effective goals and showing them how to work towards these goals is an important way to maintain persistence. Developing their self-regulatory skills can also be a means of enhancing their capacity to plan and persist in the face of a challenge. This can encompass helping them use their time more effectively, prioritising, being clear about what one is expected or required to do and developing strategies for checking that their schoolwork is done.

In terms of control, research suggests that showing students the importance of effort and effective work strategies will enhance their sense of control. Control is also developed by providing feedback in effective and consistent ways and providing task-based input on their work that focuses on how they can improve.

THE ONE ABOUT THE SPOTLIGHT EFFECT

@inner_drive | www.innerdrive.co.uk

THE STUDY

It has been said that "you'll worry less about what people think about you when you realise how seldom they do". It is easy when under pressure or stressed to believe that all eyes are on you. But are they actually, or is it just a faulty perception in your own head?

The Spotlight Effect describes the tendency for people to over-estimate how much other people notice their appearance or actions. Keen to study this in students, researchers from Cornell University collaborated in 2000 in a series of quirky and intriguing studies.

THE MAIN FINDINGS

1. In one of their studies, they had participants wear an embarrassing T-shirt to a lecture (the T-shirt of choice was one with Barry Manilow's face on it). The participants predicted that just **under half of their fellow students would notice** the T-shirt. The reality was that **less than a quarter actually did**.

2. The spotlight effect **affected all participants the same**, with no difference between male and female students.

3. The spotlight effect goes beyond just embarrassing situations, with students just as likely to **over-estimate how much people noticed them** when wearing a T-shirt of someone considered cool or iconic (in this case, Martin Luther King Jr, Bob Marley or Jerry Seinfeld).

4. Beyond just appearances, the spotlight effect was found to be **present in social situations** (both positively and negatively). Students thought that other group members would remember both their interesting points as well as their offensive ones more than they actually did.

Ref: Gilovich et al, 2000, *Journal of Personality and Social Psychology*

THE ONE ABOUT THE SPOTLIGHT EFFECT

 ## RELATED RESEARCH

Other research has found that we tend to over-emphasise the significance of our own actions. For example, one such study found that people consistently overestimate their own contributions towards a group task. Likewise, other research has found that we tend to assume that our version of reality is objective and not subjective. Finally, we tend to assume that other people will have the same perception as ourselves. These three factors combined can lead to a wide variation in how two people interpret the same event.

Most of this research has been conducted with children and is labelled "theory of mind". This describes how some people struggle to understand that others have different beliefs, knowledge and intentions than themselves. This study advances our understanding of this phenomenon by a) applying it to older students and b) adding a social status element to it.

PARENTING IMPLICATIONS

The authors of the study reflected that "people seem to believe that the social spotlight shines more brightly on them than it truly does". What impact does this have on children? "Individuals do not reach out to others because of a fear of rejection and how it will be perceived; people do not dance, sing, play a musical instrument, or join in the organisation's softball game because of the fear that they will look bad". In a school setting, these examples could easily be students not asking a question in class for fear of looking dumb, not auditioning for the school play because of fear of rejection or feeling anxious about public speaking because of fear of embarrassing themselves in front of their peers.

The researchers conclude their paper by stating: "the present research suggests that a great many of these fears may be misplaced or exaggerated. Other people may be less likely to notice or remember our shortcomings than we typically expect". Parents can help their children overcome the spotlight by normalising their worries, by explaining and demonstrating that everyone suffers from the Spotlight Effect and by creating a home environment where mistakes are used as foundation for future learning and performance.

THE ONE ABOUT DEVELOPING RESILIENCE

@inner_drive | www.innerdrive.co.uk

THE STUDY

There is a growing interest amongst teachers, schools, policy makers and parents in how best to develop resilience in young people. With increasing uncertainty in society and more pressures in the lives of young people, this area is of great importance. But how does one go about developing resilience? What does a research-informed and evidence-based programme look like?

Researchers recently reviewed the existing studies to come up with the most comprehensive set of suggestions to date.

THE MAIN FINDINGS

Creating a programme that develops and enhances resilience should focus on three distinct areas: **personal qualities**, a **facilitative environment** and **challenge mindset**.

1 Personal qualities
These include but are not limited to:

▸ **High personal standards**
▸ **Optimism**
▸ **Competitiveness**
▸ **Intrinsic motivation**
▸ **Self-confidence**
▸ **Self-talk**
▸ **Focusing on what is important and what you can control**

2 A facilitative environment
Ensuring both high levels of challenge and support.

Where resilience happens

Unrelenting	**Facilitative**
Stagnant	**Comfortable**

CHALLENGE

SUPPORT

3 A challenge mindset
Seeing things as a challenge, not a threat. This can be done by:

▸ **Focusing on what you stand to gain**
▸ **Asking yourself "what can I do about this?"**
▸ **Not catastrophising**
▸ **Avoiding words like "should" and "must"**
▸ **Concentrating on positive and helpful thoughts**

Ref: Fletcher and Sarkar, 2016, *Journal of Sport Psychology in Action*

THE ONE ABOUT DEVELOPING RESILIENCE

 ## RELATED RESEARCH

The authors of this study are amongst the leading experts on resilience. Interestingly, some of their work to date has focused on how Olympic gold medalists developed their resilience. They found that athletes who viewed their decisions as active choices and not as sacrifices, as well as those who viewed setbacks as opportunities for growth, were more resilient.

Other strategies that these Olympians used included accessing support from those around them, identifying their motivation for succeeding and drawing their confidence from a range of sources (i.e., not just their last results). The same researchers have also investigated resilience in the work-place and have made similar findings.

PARENTING IMPLICATIONS

Often with psychological interventions, it is not the "what" but the "how" that matters. Helping others develop resilience in children needs to be packaged in a way that puts them at ease and is not perceived either as punishment or because they aren't good enough. The authors of the study allude to this, and offer a potential solution, when they write:

> Because misunderstandings exist about resilience, training in this area should begin with an explanation of what resilience is and is not. It should be emphasised that feeling vulnerable to stress or struggling to cope with adversity should not be perceived as weakness. Rather, open discussion about this topic is a sign of strength and the potential beginning of positive change that will hopefully lead to individuals withstanding - and potentially thriving on - pressure.

Once this has been done, then "all three areas - personal qualities, facilitative environment and challenge mindset - need to be appropriately addressed to enhance performers' ability to withstand pressure". This three-pronged approach will ensure that individual skills, a home environment and personal mindset are all conducive to developing resilience. If this is ensured, then it is more likely that our children will develop the key skills and attributes needed to thrive both in and outside of school.

THE ONE ABOUT PHONES AND SLEEP

@inner_drive | www.innerdrive.co.uk

THE STUDY

Many of us use our mobile phones and tablets just before going to and whilst in bed. What impact does this have on our brain? Melatonin, often referred to as "the sleep hormone", is released when it is dark at night and acts as a trigger for us to feel sleepy. But does the glare from our electronics trick our brain into thinking it is daytime and stop melatonin being fully secreted?

Researchers recently ran a study to find out. Their participants started using their tablets at 11 pm and were told they could engage in whatever task they liked on them, such as reading, gaming or shopping. Then, at midnight and at 1 am, saliva samples were taken to check their melatonin levels.

THE MAIN FINDINGS

1 Being on an iPad for one hour at night hardly impacts how much melatonin is released.

The researchers do note "that usage of self-luminous electronic devices before sleep may disrupt sleep even if melatonin is not supressed. Clearly the tasks themselves may be alerting or stressful *stimuli* that can lead to sleep disruption".

2 However, being on your iPad for two hours before bed resulted in around **20%** less melatonin being released.

Therefore, they recommend "that these devices by dimmed at night as much as possible in order to minimise melatonin suppression, and that the duration of use be limited prior to bedtime".

Ref: Wood et al, 2013, *Applied Ergonomics*

THE ONE ABOUT PHONES AND SLEEP

 ## RELATED RESEARCH

A recent report found that there are now more mobile phones on the planet than people, with one survey finding that 81% of people report never turning their phone off – even when they are in bed. Another study found that on average, people check their devices 85 times a day, with many in this study being unaware of how often they do so.

More and more research is being conducted on the link between electronic devices and sleep (#71). One such study found that being on your phone within an hour of bed means that you are almost three times as likely to get less than five hours of sleep. As well as the obvious suggestion of not being on your phone whilst in bed, a different study found another good way to minimise the negative impact was to turn down the backlight and hold your phone more than 12 inches away from your face.

What children do on their phone will also impact the quality and length of sleep. Both social media and constantly replying to messages have been found to increase stress and reduce immunity. If people are going to be on their phone, doing something calming and relaxing on it before bed is certainly advisable.

PARENTING IMPLICATIONS

This one of the biggest and most important areas that parents can directly affect. Given the impact that mobile phones can have on how students feel, think and behave the next day, it is important to take a firm and clear line on it. What this line looks like will depend on your parenting philosophy and how much your child uses their phone – but either way, clear and consistent messages and guidelines that are enforced should be the cornerstone of any mobile phone policy at home.

The authors of the study allude to this when they write that their results are "particularly worrisome in populations such as young adults and adolescents, who already tend to be more 'night owls'". Talking to your children about the perils of being on their devices too much late at night and the consequences it has on their learning and exam performance makes sense from both a well-being and an academic achievement perspective.

THE ONE ABOUT PICTURES AND WORDS

@inner_drive | www.innerdrive.co.uk

THE STUDY

What do you think would lead to better learning: revising with just words, just pictures, words and then pictures or words and pictures together? Keen to find out, researchers investigated. Over two experiments, they had students learn about how a bike pump worked using these different techniques. Afterwards, the students took both problem-solving and verbal recall tests.

THE MAIN FINDINGS

Studying with words and pictures together was found to **lead to better learning**. Specifically, on a problem-solving test, these students:

✓ Correctly answered over twice as many questions as those who had just revised **with words**.

✓ Correctly answered over **50% more** questions than those who had revised **with just pictures**.

✓ Correctly answered around **50% more** questions than those who had revised by **seeing words followed by pictures**.

Revising with words and pictures together **did not help** when students had to verbally recall what they had studied.

The **difference came when** they had to apply this knowledge to different problems, situations and questions.

Ref: Mayer et al, 1991, *Journal of Educational Psychology*

THE ONE ABOUT PICTURES AND WORDS

 ## RELATED RESEARCH

This research lends support to a memory strategy known as "Dual-Coding", which forms a part of Cognitive Load Theory (#70). The authors of the study explain that "this theory predicts that learners will remember and transfer material better if they encode the material both visually and verbally because they have two separate ways of finding the information in their memory".

Therefore, when students study using both words and pictures, this builds both verbal and visual representations of the material, as well as strengthening the connection between the two. This process cements information into long-term memory.

Research into Dual-Coding has found that it enhances memory and learning for primary, secondary and university students. Furthermore, this effect has been found in both laboratory studies and in real-world settings (i.e., in schools), as well as in a range of subjects.

PARENTING IMPLICATIONS

Many students use a range of techniques to help them remember large amounts of material. This may include writing out their notes or producing mind-maps. This study - and, indeed, the theory - suggests that this may be an incomplete strategy. As the authors of the study state, "even when instruction involves both words and pictures, our results show that presenting verbal and visual explanations without connecting them is much less helpful than coordinating verbal narration simultaneously with animation". Clearly, doing both simultaneously is far more effective than doing one after the other.

A good way to encourage your children to start using Dual-Coding is to consider what words they could write down to describe a visual graphic, or what graphic would capture the core message from the text. Key to this is understanding what type of visuals may go best with the text for each subject or topic. The more congruent the text description and visual graphic are, the more likely these will lead to deeper learning.

THE ONE ABOUT TEACHING OTHERS

@inner_drive | www.innerdrive.co.uk

THE STUDY

What are the best conditions for learning and revision? Does it help motivate people to know that they have an upcoming test? Or is it more beneficial to tell students that they are going to have to teach the material to one of their peers?

These were the questions that researchers sought to answer. Across two experiments, they split 100 students into two groups (teach others versus prepare for a test). They then measured what they learnt, how much they learnt and how well they did in a test.

THE MAIN FINDINGS

1 Students **who had been expecting to teach** the material to someone else remembered more of the material and **did so in a more efficient way** than those who thought there was going to be a test.

2 In their final exam, those **who had expected to teach someone** performed over **12% better** than those who were working towards the test.

3 As well as remembering more and performing better in tests, **students who thought that they were going to teach someone** were also **more likely to remember** the important information and key topics.

Ref: Nestojko et al, 2014, *Memory and Cognition*

THE ONE ABOUT TEACHING OTHERS

 ## RELATED RESEARCH

Numerous studies have found that when students teach material to other students, they make significant learning gains. In the research, this is known as the Protégé Effect. However, it is worth noting that not all studies have shown this effect. Reasons for these mixed findings may include the increase in anxiety and stress in some students when they must speak in public. This would suggest that anything we can do to help minimise anxiety or stress around speaking in public should help.

Related research, known as the Production Effect (#65), supports the idea of teaching others to improve memory, as it states that if students produce something new from the learning material (i.e., a new lesson for someone else) then this will help ingrain the material in their long-term memory. Essentially, creating something prompts students to think harder and deeper about the content.

PARENTING IMPLICATIONS

The researchers note that "instilling an expectation to teach seems to be a simple, inexpensive intervention with the potential to increase learning efficiency at home and in the classroom". Why is this effective? They explain that:

> Participants expecting to teach put themselves into the mindset of a teacher, leading them to adopt certain effective strategies used by teaching when preparing to teach - such as organizing and weighing the importance of different concepts in the to-be-taught material, focusing on the main points and thinking about how information fits together.

Therefore, if your child expects that they will have teach you some of the content that they are learning, it will prompt them to categorise the important information and will encourage them to go over what they do and don't know thoroughly in preparation for tough questions. Expecting to teach others is so effective because it encourages both self-explanation (prompting detail and depth) and elaborative interrogation (asking yourself "why is this the case?") (#23). Both of these techniques are regularly associated with higher levels of understanding and memory retention.

THE ONE ABOUT EXPERTS OVERCLAIMING

@inner_drive | www.innerdrive.co.uk

THE STUDY

Many people tend to overestimate their knowledge, skills and abilities. If we believe ourselves to be experts in one area, are we more likely to exaggerate what we actually know? Researchers from Cornell University and Tulane University ran a series of studies to find out.

To give an example of how they tested this, they asked people to rate how familiar they were with a list of key terms. Unbeknownst to those being studied, some of the terms were real and some were fake. For example, in the banking section, real terms included "fixed-rate mortgage" and "home equity" and false ones "pre-rated stocks" and "annualized credit".

THE MAIN FINDINGS

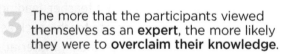

1 Over **90% of the participants** claimed to have at least **some knowledge** of some of the made-up phrases.

2 Those **who had done well** in an easy quiz and thus felt more like an expert about a topic were subsequently **more likely to overclaim** their knowledge.

3 The more that the participants viewed themselves as an **expert**, the more likely they were to **overclaim their knowledge**.

4 This effect of experts overclaiming was found to be **true in a range of studies** and topics, which included science, geography, banking and literature.

5 Even if participants **had been warned** that some of the information they were about to read **was false**, many of them still overclaimed their knowledge about these topics.

Ref: Atir et al, 2015, *Psychological Science*

THE ONE ABOUT EXPERTS OVERCLAIMING

 RELATED RESEARCH

Other research has shown that people are not very accurate at predicting their own ability levels. To date, this has focused on either novices or people who aren't particularly accomplished at the task at hand overestimating their abilities. This is referred to as the Dunning-Kruger Effect (#16).

Further research has also found that the allure of expertise and authority means that people are sometimes seduced by false information. This is one of the reasons why people tend to believe things if they sound scientific – even if they are false.

A different study recently looked at the other costs of being an expert. They found that people who consider themselves to be an expert are also more likely to be close-minded, refusing to change their original opinion when new and contradictory evidence is presented. This is a form of confirmation bias which occurs because people want to appear to be consistent with their earlier thoughts, beliefs and actions (#38).

PARENTING IMPLICATIONS

The authors of this study caution about the pitfalls of experts overclaiming by saying that "a tendency to over claim may discourage individuals from educating themselves in precisely those areas in which they consider themselves knowledgeable and that may be important to them". Steve Jobs, founder of Apple, once alluded to this by advising people to "stay hungry, stay foolish".

If students believe they are already experts, this can lead to them developing a fixed mindset and not seeking out opportunities to develop and improve. Having a fixed mindset has been associated with lower grades, poorer coping skills and reduced mental health (#56). Parents can help guard against this by consistently encouraging students to do challenging work that stretches them and providing feedback that is both regular and focused on concrete steps to get better. This will help protect students against what they say is "the great menace – not ignorance, but the illusion of knowledge".

THE ONE ABOUT THE IKEA EFFECT

@inner_drive | www.innerdrive.co.uk

THE STUDY

The IKEA Effect describes how some people overvalue their own ideas, efforts and creations compared to the equivalent done by others. This phenomenon, named after the Swedish furniture store that requires you to assemble your own furniture, partly explains why some people are married to their ideas, over-estimate the quality of their efforts and place more value than others do on the things that they have worked hard on. This may be why some people struggle to, in the words of the animated film *Frozen*, "let it go".

Researchers from Harvard Business School, Tulane University and Duke University ran a series of studies to find out how prevalent the IKEA Effect is.

THE MAIN FINDINGS

1 Half the participants built an IKEA piece of furniture, whereas the other half inspected an identical piece once it had already been assembled. They each then estimated the price of it. Those **who had built** the furniture themselves **valued it at 63% more** expensive.

2 People **who had built** their own furniture were also more likely to report **liking their furniture more**.

3 This finding was replicated with participants who **made their own origami**, as they were prepared to pay **nearly five times more** than their counterparts who had not been involved in making it.

4 When comparing **their own piece of work** with that of experts, participants placed a similar value on their work if they had **worked hard** on creating it themselves.

5 Finally, in a separate study, participants were **more likely to place a higher value** on a Lego toy if **a)** it was theirs and **b)** they had built it.

Ref: Norton et al, 2011, *Journal of Consumer Psychology*

THE ONE ABOUT THE IKEA EFFECT

RELATED RESEARCH

There is not a lot of related research on this topic as it is a relatively new area in psychology. This means that it would be good if these results are tested and replicated again on a different type of sample and in a range of settings.

The nearest related research falls into one of two categories. The first is "effort justification" which found that the worse an initiation into a club, the more that members tended to feel it was worth it. This suggests that they wanted to believe their efforts were justified. This finding, curiously, has been replicated in studies on rats and birds, with both types of animals preferring food that they had to work hard to get.

The other area in psychology which is like the IKEA Effect is confirmation bias. This is the tendency to prefer information and ideas that you have previously agreed with. The need to feel consistent with our prior activities drives how we feel about a new situation.

PARENTING IMPLICATIONS

There is obviously nothing wrong with encouraging children to value their efforts and hard work. The problem comes with the disconnect between what they and others see. The researchers summed this up well by using the metaphor of selling your house: "for instance, people may see the improvements they have made to their homes - such as the brick walkway they laid by hand - as increasing the value of the house far more than buyers, who only see a shoddily built walkway".

This helps explain why some people have a hard time letting go of their "brilliant idea". This leads to them persisting long after they should have quit and come up with a better one. It is like the gambler's equivalent of throwing good money after bad. This can be compounded by frustration when others do not see the value of your suggestions. Although resilience and persistence clearly are admirable traits, knowing that students have a bias to their own work, ideas and effort can help save everyone time and money if we are able to help them accurately assess the value of their ideas.

THE ONE ABOUT PARENTAL BELIEFS

@inner_drive | www.innerdrive.co.uk

THE STUDY

Maths is a subject that students tend to have very strong opinions about one way or another. One of the most important and interesting studies on parental beliefs and their impact on how students view their maths ability was conducted over 30 years ago.

In this study, researchers from The University of Michigan administered a series of questionnaires to children aged 10-15 years old and their parents. They wanted to see how powerful parental attitudes and expectations were and if these varied between parents of sons and parents of daughters.

THE MAIN FINDINGS

1 A child's opinion of their own ability and expectation of future success was **heavily shaped** by what their parents thought about them.

This actually had more impact than the child's previous grades in that subject. Essentially, they **believe their parents more** than their grades.

2 Out of the two, the **attitudes and beliefs of mothers** towards their child's educational abilities had **more impact** than the father's.

3 Parents of daughters thought that **maths was harder** for their child and that they would have to **work harder to do well** in it compared to parents of sons. This belief was held by both mothers and fathers.

4 Parents of sons thought **advanced maths** was more important for their child than parents of daughters.

Ref: Parson et al, 1982, *Child Development*

THE ONE ABOUT PARENTAL BELIEFS

RELATED RESEARCH

Recent research has focused on which parental attitudes and behaviours are most likely to help students get better grades. The most significant by far were having high academic expectations (#9). This included how important parents considered school to be, their attitude towards teachers and the overall value they placed on education. Other good strategies included regular communication, encouraging good reading habits (#46) and setting clear boundaries and structure for managing homework and social leisure time.

Previous evidence suggests that parents tend to have subconscious bias towards their beliefs about what different genders can achieve in school, with several studies finding higher expectations for boys once they are in the latter stages of their education. Indeed, it is interesting to note that one study (#17) found that parents were more than twice as likely to praise their sons for their effort than their daughters. Perhaps this explains why other studies have found that girls think they have to work harder at maths than boys do, even though both boys and girls report spending similar amounts of time doing their homework.

PARENTING IMPLICATIONS

The authors of the study point out that the main finding of their study is that "parental beliefs are even more critical mediators than the child's own maths performance" and that "by attributing their daughter's achievements to hard work and their son's to high ability, parents may be teaching their sons and daughters to draw different inferences regarding their achievement abilities".

This means that each time a parent says that their child "isn't a maths person" it can have a very serious and negative impact on the child's beliefs about their maths potential. This suggests that raising aspirations and expectations would be a productive strategy. The key to doing so is to aim for challenging but realistic expectations. This sets the bar high enough to improve performance whilst also ensuring that the child feels it is attainable, as it is within reach of their abilities.

THE ONE ABOUT MOTIVATION

@inner_drive | www.innerdrive.co.uk

THE STUDY

If you had to learn a new topic that was taught in the most boring of ways, what do you think would be the best way to motivate yourself? Researchers from the University of Iowa and the University of Oklahoma divided students into four groups to find out. The first was not given a reason to try hard. The second was told about an important test on the topic. The third group was told that trying hard was what they "should" do as it was expected of them, and finally the fourth group was told that they would be learning a new skill that would help them in the future.

THE MAIN FINDINGS

The fourth group, with an emphasis on developing skills for their future, performed better on a range of measures. Specifically:

- ✓ They **rated the lesson as more important**. In some cases, this difference was **up to 25% more** than in the other three groups.

- ✓ They had **higher levels of self-determination**, that is, **an increase** in more internal motivation.

- ✓ They were **far more likely** to put in more effort in the lesson. Knowing that there **would be a test**, that it was expected of them or no reason resulted in a lot less effort.

Effort Versus Why

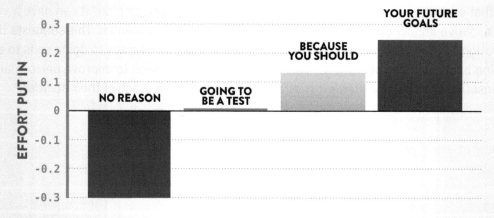

Ref: Reeve et al, 2004, *Motivation and Emotion*

THE ONE ABOUT MOTIVATION

 ## RELATED RESEARCH

There has been a plethora of research on how best to enhance motivation (#47). One fascinating paper found that individual motivation can be improved if the person felt that they had a reasonable amount of choice over what they did or how they did it, if they knew why they were doing it and if quality feedback was offered. Other research has shown that if people feel that they are getting better or learning new things, then their motivation levels will remain constant and high.

Other ways to boost motivation levels can be found in research around goal-setting. If done correctly, in a way that is both challenging and realistic as well as process-focused, it can increase concentration as well as the likelihood of students choosing challenging tasks. As a result, initial performance improves, which creates a positive cycle of even higher motivation levels and better subsequent performances.

PARENTING IMPLICATIONS

Helping children maintain their motivation levels is a problem that every parent encounters. Instead of seeing motivation as something you give someone, it is better to see motivation as something that you can help develop. This research gives an indication of how this can be done. Clearly, emphasising the importance of an upcoming test can help provide a short-term boost before an event, but doing so is unlikely to help foster the intrinsic motivation needed for students to learn a large amount of material over a sustained period of time.

The authors of this study do note that "it would be a misrepresentation of our findings to conclude that simply telling another person that an activity is useful will lead them to identify with its personal value". Understanding why an activity is important and helping students identify how it will directly help to them, as well as how it will help them achieve their goals, is a much more effective approach to facilitating meaningful motivation.

THE ONE ABOUT STUDENT DAYDREAMING

@inner_drive | www.innerdrive.co.uk

THE STUDY

Sometimes it is obvious, but sometimes it is hard to spot when students are daydreaming. So, how prevalent is mind wandering in class, when is it most likely to occur and what are the costs of doing so?

Researchers from the University of Waterloo in Canada tracked 154 students over the course of a 12-week term. At various random stages in their lectures, they were asked to rate their levels of concentration and report on what they had just been focusing on. Their results allow us to know more than ever before how much attention students really pay in class.

THE MAIN FINDINGS

1 Students' minds **wandered for a third** of their lectures. **14%** of the time was spent unintentionally daydreaming, and **20%** of the time students actively chose to think about things other than the lecture.

2 Attention levels **don't linearly decrease** during a 50-minute lecture. Interestingly, attention levels were actually **lower in the third quarter** than they were in the fourth quarter.

3 Students' minds were most likely to wander on **a Monday** and **a Friday**. They were at their **most focused** on **Wednesdays**.

The researchers speculated that this was due to them either worrying about the upcoming week or being distracted by thoughts about the weekend.

4 During lessons towards the end of term, students were far **more likely** to report being distracted in their lessons. One possible reason for this could be that **their minds were on upcoming exams** and the potential consequences of not doing well in the exam.

5 Unsurprisingly, the more students reported daydreaming, the worse they did in their exams. This was **true for all students** regardless of their previous academic performance.

Ref: Wammes et al, 2016, *Scholarship of Teaching and Learning in Psychology*

THE ONE ABOUT STUDENT DAYDREAMING

RELATED RESEARCH

One of the first reported studies in this area, conducted in the 1970s, had students report on what they were focusing on every time their teacher rang a bell. Amazingly, students reported not focusing on the task at hand in lessons for the same amount of time as the students in this study conducted more than 40 years later. Both sets of students reported focusing on something that wasn't to do with the lesson 33% of the time.

What can be done to reduce the time spent not focusing on the task at hand? Some researchers have hypothesised a link between motivation and daydreaming in which increasing the former reduces the latter. Indeed, the authors of the study note that:

> Mind wandering of the intentional sort might be curtailed through interventions that increase students' motivation to perform, or their perceived value of attending to the lecture material. One way to increase students' motivation to attend might be to include quiz questions in the lecture, with the accuracy of the students' responses counting toward their final grade.

PARENTING IMPLICATIONS

What can parents do differently given the results of this study? Since students are more likely to be distracted on Mondays and Fridays, the authors of the study suggest that "instructors might consider presenting a greater volume of material, or presenting the most important material midweek". Therefore, parents could encourage students to do the most difficult and cognitively demanding homework tasks midweek.

This study highlights the importance of student concentration. Other research suggests that practical tips to help encourage better focus include getting a good night's sleep regularly, eating breakfast every morning, drinking plenty of water, regular exercise (#42), taking notes in class (#27) and turning mobile phones off. If we can explicitly teach these techniques to our children, we can arm them with a wider range of strategies that they can employ to increase their focus during their learning.

THE ONE ABOUT GOING FOR A WALK

@inner_drive | www.innerdrive.co.uk

THE STUDY

The classical Greek physician Hippocrates once stated that "if you are in a bad mood, go for a walk. If you are still in a bad mood, go for another walk". So, does going for a walk actually help improve mood? What if you know you have to do a really hard and boring task afterwards? And how short does a "short walk" have to be for people to get any psychological benefit from it?

Across three experiments, researchers Jeffrey Miller and Zlatan Krizan of Iowa State University sought to find out.

THE MAIN FINDINGS

1 Students who went for a **12-minute walk** reported **feeling much better** (i.e., around a 20% increase) than those who had spent **the same amount of time sitting down** looking at photos. This included feelings of happiness, attentiveness and confidence.

2 Students who knew they had to do a **hard and boring task afterwards**, still **had a positive mood boost** as a result of their walk. Those who had been sitting down instead **did not**.

3 Participants who took part in a really short walk, **lasting only 5 minutes**, still got the benefits and reported **feeling better** afterwards.

4 Having a walking break **doesn't even need to involve going outside** to feel the benefits. Students who went for a short walk inside felt **better afterwards**. Students who stood still or sat down reported **feeling worse**.

Ref: Miller and Krizan, 2016, *Emotion*

THE ONE ABOUT GOING FOR A WALK

 ## RELATED RESEARCH

There is a lot of emerging research that highlights the many and varied benefits of physical activity. For example, researchers have found that those who exercise regularly cope better with stressful situations and report feeling more focused and alert on days that they exercised. Likewise, a recent study found that students who exercised up to four hours after a lesson were able to later recall and retain more information than those who did not.

The long-term effects of exercise are also well known now. These include, but are not limited to, enhanced cognitive functions, physical health benefits and feeling more refreshed. Where you go for a walk may also matter, with recent evidence suggesting that those who do so in natural environments get an extra boost compared with those who do so in urban environments (#50). This is because urban environments require individuals to stay alert, negating some of the positive psychological impacts of going for a walk.

PARENTING IMPLICATIONS

This study could prove useful in helping parents enhance the mood and well-being of their children. This may be why going for "learning walks" or breaking up study sessions with a quick stroll may help. So, why don't students do this more? The researchers note that "people may underestimate the extent to which just getting off their couch and going for a walk will benefit their mood as they focus on momentarily perceived barriers rather than eventual mood benefits".

The results from this study could not be clearer, in that "walking has powerful and ongoing consequences on our mental states, and these should be harnessed to improve wellbeing and performance". What is good to know is that this evidence shows that it does not have to be a long walk. Even 5-10 minutes could provide just the pick-me-up that students need for the rest of the day.

THE ONE ABOUT STRESS MINDSETS

@inner_drive | www.innerdrive.co.uk

THE STUDY

It is a myth that stress is always bad. It is probably more accurate to portray it in terms of the "Goldilocks effect" – too much or too little is not helpful. If there is enough to motivate a person and yet not so much that it hinders useful behaviours, then clear thinking and performance can improve.

Central to this may be how individuals interpret stress. Some view stress as always being a bad thing, whereas others view it as having some potential benefit. This is known as your "stress mindset". Researchers from Yale University ran a study to test if a "stress mindset" was actually a real thing and if so, what impact it had.

THE MAIN FINDINGS

1 Stress can be viewed in **one of two ways**: either with the potential to **enhance or debilitate** performance.

2 Our **stress mindset** can be developed. Learning how it can help us is key.

3 Those who view stress as being helpful reported:
- ✔ **Feeling better**
- ✔ **Better work performance**
- ✔ **Being more likely to seek out feedback**

4 If participants had **high levels of cortisol,** the stress hormone, then a belief that stress can be good for you **helped lower it.**

If participants **had low levels of cortisol,** then believing stress can be good for you **helped raise it.** Essentially, it helped participants find their **sweet spot.**

Ref: Crum et al, 2013, *Journal of Personality and Social Psychology*

THE ONE ABOUT STRESS MINDSETS

 ## RELATED RESEARCH

Research has identified that stress plays a role in the six main causes of death (heart disease, accidents, cancer, liver disease, lung ailments and suicide). It is also associated with sick days and a reduction in productivity, depression and general reduction in performance. However, it is worth noting that in evolutionary terms, stress played a key role in our survival, as it helped our ancestors run faster and think more quickly under pressure. A little bit of stress can also help people learn and perform more effectively (#51).

The benefits of stress have been studied from two different viewpoints: the physiological and the psychological. From a physiological perspective, evidence shows that an appropriate amount of stress elicits the release of certain hormones that can help repair cells and can make the body stronger and healthier. Likewise, several researchers have found that individuals report having more meaning to their lives and developing resilience, a new sense of perspective and better relationships as a result of experiencing stressful situations. This has been dubbed "stress related growth".

PARENTING IMPLICATIONS

This study does not suggest that more stress is better or that there are no downsides to experiencing stress. Instead, what the authors of the study point out is that "the findings of these studies indicate that people can be primed to adopt a 'stress-is-enhancing' mindset, which can have positive consequences relating to improved health and work performance".

This suggests that during times of heightened stress - for example, exam time or during public speaking - parents need to help students develop three things. Firstly, ensure that they have a large skill and knowledge base from which to draw. The more competent someone is at something, the less likely they are to become stressed whilst doing it. Secondly, self-regulation skills, such as managing their focus and how they talk to themselves, can help them deliver their best under pressure. Thirdly and finally, that one's stress mindset is not set in stone. Focusing on how to interpret both the event itself and one's attitude to stress can significantly reduce one's negative feelings whilst boosting performance.

THE ONE ABOUT HOW TO GIVE BETTER FEEDBACK

@inner_drive | www.innerdrive.co.uk

THE STUDY

Given the amount of time, energy and effort that is invested into giving feedback, it would be handy to know what good feedback actually looks like. Researchers John Hattie and Helen Timperley from the University of Auckland conducted a thorough review of the existing research. Their findings offer simple tips, strategies and guidelines on what may work best.

THE MAIN FINDINGS

1 In order to be most effective, feedback must answer three questions:

Where am I going?
This makes your goal crystal clear.

How am I going?
This gives an indication of progress.

Where to next?
Perhaps the most important question, as it focuses on strategies needed in order to improve.

2 They also identified four types of feedback and commented on their effectiveness:

Feedback about the person
This is **the least effective** as it leads to labelling, such as "you are smart" or "you are not a maths person", neither of which is particularly helpful.

Feedback about the task
This is the most common and provides information on whether the work was correct. **This is often effective** if students had a faulty interpretation of what was needed.

Feedback about the process
Provides information on how the students did the task. It prompts them to search out more information and **often leads to deeper learning** than just feedback on the task.

Feedback about self-regulation
This covers how well students monitored their performance, regulated their actions and tweaked their strategies. This is more **effective for novice learners.**

Ref: Hattie and Timperley, 2007, *Review of Educational Research*

THE ONE ABOUT HOW TO GIVE BETTER FEEDBACK

 ## RELATED RESEARCH

One famous review on feedback studies found that 38% of feedback interventions actually do more harm than good. As a result, this topic has been studied extensively. It is just too important to get wrong or to not know its potential implications.

One study found that a quarter of teenager students prefer to be praised loudly and publicly, whereas two thirds of students preferred it if the teacher did it quietly and discreetly. Several other researchers have found that if feedback is merged with praise, it can have a detrimental effect if delivered in the presence of one's friends who do not value hard work and doing well at school.

A different study confirmed these findings and found that students preferred praise for their efforts over their natural abilities. This sort of feedback is associated with students enjoying a task more, enhancing their own resilience and choosing more challenging tasks in the future (#5).

PARENTING IMPLICATIONS

For better tips on giving good feedback, the authors of the study recommend two separate but inter-related strategies. The first is that "feedback is more effective when it provides information on correct rather than incorrect responses and when it builds on changes from previous trials". The second is that feedback is "more effective when there are perceived low rather than high levels of threat to self-esteem, presumably because low-threat conditions allow attention to be paid to the feedback".

This research paper is gold dust for parents considering how much time and energy is spent giving their children feedback. These strategies suggest that it is about quality rather than quantity. Or, as the researchers state, "simply providing more feedback is not the answer, because it is necessary to consider the nature of the feedback, the timing, and how a student receives this feedback".

THE ONE ABOUT ABOUT SELF-TALK

@inner_drive | www.innerdrive.co.uk

THE STUDY

What do Donald Trump, Zlatan Ibrahimovic, Julius Caesar and Elmo from Sesame Street all have in common? They are all known to talk about themselves in the third person. One famous example of this was when Zlatan Ibrahimovic was invited to a trial at Arsenal. He replied, "Zlatan doesn't do auditions".

But what impact does how you talk to yourself have on how you think, feel and behave? Does talking in the first person (i.e. "I thought that . . .") differ when compared to non-first person (i.e., "You thought that . . ." or using your own name in the third person)? Researchers had students talk to themselves in one of these two ways and then put them in a range of situations that included recalling bad events, meeting someone for the first time and giving a presentation in front of their peers.

THE MAIN FINDINGS

People who talked to themselves in the first person compared to non-first person

✓ Felt **more emotional** intensity when recalling an event that made them **anxious**

✓ Felt **more emotional** intensity when recalling an event that made them **angry**

✓ Were rated as **appearing more nervous** and **performed worse** in social interactions

✓ Were **less likely** to make a good **first impression**

✓ Experienced more **shame, embarrassment** and **negative moods** during a public speaking task

✓ **Performed worse** at the public speaking task

✓ Were **more likely** to see upcoming stressful events as a **threat**

✓ Were **more likely** to **worry** about upcoming stressful events

Ref: Kross et al, 2014, *Journal of Personality and Social Psychology*

THE ONE ABOUT SELF-TALK

 ## RELATED RESEARCH

The area of self-talk is one of the most well-researched and robust areas in cognitive psychology (#21). How one talks to oneself has been found to impact one's mindset, motivation, resilience, creativity, concentration, emotional control and metacognitive abilities. For example, one study found that participants who asked themselves questions (i.e., "Will I do well?") solved far more anagrams than those who had declared they would succeed (i.e., "I will do well"). One possible reason for this is that asking yourself questions helps prompt the brain to answer questions, functioning as a call to action (#23).

Other studies have found that telling yourself what to do in a helpful and constructive manner improves attention and performance under pressure. This technique also has been found to help students improve self-control as well as boost their planning and preparation before an important task. Finally, upbeat and energised self-talk has been found to help people block out potentially distracting thoughts. This helps improve performance when a large amount of effort and resilience is required.

PARENTING IMPLICATIONS

This research shows the numerous benefits of developing how children talk to themselves. The authors conclude their findings by stating that:

> We are not accustomed to people referring to themselves using their own name – the current findings suggest that doing so promotes self-distancing; enhances people's ability to regulate their thoughts, feelings and behaviours under social stress; and leads them to appraise social-anxiety-provoking events in more challenging and less threatening terms.

Given the advantages associated with this type of self-talk, it is interesting to consider how little time is actually spent on helping students develop a healthy and helpful self-narrative. A few simple little tweaks can really have a big impact on how they think, feel and behave. Given that self-regulation and emotional management are key day-to-day skills (#31), helping our children develop their self-talk skills promises to be a simple and effective strategy to boost their well-being and achievement.

THE ONE ABOUT PARENTS AND READING

@inner_drive | www.innerdrive.co.uk

THE STUDY

Parents are often advised to read to their children as part of a night-time routine. But is there a way that they can do this to best develop the reading skills of their children?

Researchers tracked children ages 4 to 6 years old for several years and measured how much parents reported reading to them, what type of reading activities they participated in and then measured key literacy skills. The researchers defined two distinct reading practices that parents participate in. These were informal interactions (i.e., reading storybooks) and formal interactions (i.e., teaching different letter names and sounds). They tested to see if these two different strategies played an important and distinct role in developing literacy skills.

THE MAIN FINDINGS

1 **"Informal interactions"**, such as reading storybooks, had a **positive impact** on their child's abilty a year later to:

✓ **Understand words and sentences**

✓ **Use a wider range of vocabulary**

✓ **Develop listening comprehension skills**

2 **Teaching children** about letters, words and sentences during reading (i.e., formal interactions) was also found to play a role in **developing early literacy skills**.

3 The **amount of books** that children were exposed to by age 6 was a **positive predictor** of their reading ability two years later.

Ref: Senechal and LeFevre, 2002, *Child Development*

THE ONE ABOUT PARENTS AND READING

 ## RELATED RESEARCH

The positive effects of reading storybooks to children have long been established. It is interesting to note that research indicates that many children enjoy this time with their parents, with many children often initiating joint reading time together. Children's interest in reading books has been linked to their reading abilities at a younger age. This suggests that if we want to develop a love of reading in our children, it is important that we help them develop their competence and confidence levels early.

One related study found that it is not just the quantity of reading that parents do with their child that matters, but also the quality of the interactions during that time. This includes both describing what is happening in the book, but also putting on a little performance whilst doing so.

PARENTING IMPLICATIONS

A recent study found that students who are behind on their reading age when they are 9 are four times less likely to graduate high school. This emphasises the importance of helping children develop these key skills early. Essentially, if students come to school without the tools needed to learn, although it is possible for them to catch up, it makes their educational experience far more challenging.

The key takeaway for parents seems to be a combination of both formal and informal interactions during reading activities, as this can help play a big role in a child's eventual reading ability. This emphasis on both quality and quantity, as well as varying the types of activities, can offer parents a good starting point. Other tips include selecting age-appropriate books as well as using lots of questions and prompts during reading sessions to help ensure maximum interaction, engagement and learning.

THE ONE ABOUT DEADLINES, PROCRASTINATION AND CHOICE

@inner_drive | www.innerdrive.co.uk

THE STUDY

Are students prepared to set self-imposed deadlines to help themselves overcome their procrastination? Do they set effective deadlines for themselves? And do these self-imposed deadlines actually help improve their performance?

To investigate these questions, researchers divided students into two groups. In the first group, students got to set their own deadlines for three pieces of work. In the other, the teacher set the deadlines and did so evenly over the course of the term. They then tracked how the students got on.

In a follow-up study, they replicated these conditions with students who had to proofread someone else's work. Again, some of these students chose their own deadlines whereas others had deadlines imposed upon them.

THE MAIN FINDINGS

1 Perhaps unsurprisingly, a lot of students decided to submit all three assignments in the **last week of term**, with **27%** of students deciding to submit all three assignment on the **very last day** of term.

2 Students who chose their own deadlines got **lower marks** than those who had been set the deadlines by their teacher.

3 **The biggest difference** between the **student-set deadline** and **teacher-set deadline** was for the third and final piece of work, with almost **10%** difference between the two groups.

This was because if students handed in all three pieces of work at the end of the term, **they were often left with too little time** to do the final assignment.

4 Students **preferred to choose their own deadlines**, even though this ended up leading to worse overall grades.

5 Students who were set deadlines reported **spending more time on the tasks** compared to students who got to choose their own deadlines.

Ref: Ariely and Weternbroch, 2002, *Psychological Science*

THE ONE ABOUT DEADLINES, PROCRASTINATION AND CHOICE

 ## RELATED RESEARCH

Procrastination is a big problem for many students. Previous research has found that 75% of students consider themselves procrastinators, with 50% doing so regularly and to a level that is considered problematic. One reason why students may procrastinate is because people often are poor at predicting how long a task will take and will often underestimate the time needed to complete it. This is known as "The Planning Fallacy" (#3).

Other research has focused on not just the cost of procrastination, but the behaviours and thought processes associated with it. This includes low self-esteem, irrational beliefs, a high fear of failure, depression, poor study habits and too much time spent daydreaming about being successful (#53). Furthermore, those who procrastinate have been found to be more stressed and likely to be ill nearer a deadline, often culminating in lower results.

The results of this study support the findings of one of the largest-ever reviews on procrastination. In that review, the researcher noted that short regular deadlines would help as "it has long been observed that the further away an event is, the less impact it has on peoples' decisions".

PARENTING IMPLICATIONS

The researchers of the study succinctly summed up their findings when they concluded that "self-imposed deadlines did not enhance performance as much as externally imposed, evenly spaced deadlines". Why might this be the case? One reason they suggest is that "it is possible that students in the free-choice section, compared with those in the no-choice section, treated these deadlines as less binding because they were self-imposed".

Parents can use this research to help ensure their children stay focused and on track, especially as they get older and need to do more independent study and research. Even if students must take more responsibility for when, where and how they do their homework, they can still be aided by parents breaking down large tasks into small chunks with regular deadlines to help them along the way.

THE ONE ABOUT SMART REPUTATIONS

THE STUDY

@inner_drive | www.innerdrive.co.uk

When children do something well or are successful, it is almost second nature to say something like "well done, you are such a smart boy" or "you're such a clever girl". But is there a cost of praising someone for their intelligence? What implications does this have for future tasks?

Researchers from universities in China, America and Canada recently collaborated on a study to find out. Working with 243 young children, they told half of them that they had a reputation for being smart. All the students played a guessing game in which there was an opportunity to cheat by peeking at the answer when the experimenter stepped outside the room. They wanted to see if having a smart reputation influenced the students' decision to cheat or not.

THE MAIN FINDINGS

1 **61**% of the students **with a smart reputation cheated** in the game, whereas **only 41**% of the other students did.

2 Even students as young as 3 years old were **more likely to cheat** if they believed others thought that they were smart.

3 Students were **more likely to cheat** if the person administering the game was the same person who told them they had a smart reputation, as they **wanted to maintain** this appearance.

4 **Boys were more likely to cheat** than girls, regardless of whether they had a smart reputation or not.

Ref: Zhao et al, 2017, *Developmental Science*

THE ONE ABOUT SMART REPUTATIONS

 ## RELATED RESEARCH

Previous research has found that students understand their reputations by the age of 5. This study suggests that it may be even earlier. It is interesting to consider that other research has found that children under the age of 7 worry less about how smart they are compared with older children. This would suggest that adults are more fascinated by how intelligent a young child is than the actual child is themselves.

Other evidence suggests that students who are praised for their natural ability or intelligence were more likely to give up on difficult tasks, enjoy the tasks less, perform worse and lie about how well they had done (#5). This has also been associated with lower self-esteem and higher levels of stress (#56).

The finding in this study that boys cheated more than girls is consistent with research in economics and psychology that found that adult males are more likely to cheat and act dishonestly than females. However, the reason for this is currently unclear and is still being investigated.

PARENTING IMPLICATIONS

The authors state that "providing positive information to children about their intellectual ability can have unintended negative consequences". This is because telling them that they are smart may "motivate them to cheat in pursuit of personal gain". What starts with the good intention of boosting a child's morale can quickly become a weight on their shoulders.

It is important that we keep children focused on improving themselves, rather than worrying about proving themselves. If their perception of winning or being smart is more important to them than getting better, then they are likely to take shortcuts and cheat to maintain that reputation. This can be the difference between students not wanting to make mistakes and wanting to improve; between not wanting to lose rather than wanting to learn and between self-protecting behaviours and self-enhancing ones. By praising children's processes and not their innate ability, we can better help them navigate through challenging times.

THE ONE ABOUT EMOTIONS AND ACHIEVEMENT

@inner_drive | www.innerdrive.co.uk

THE STUDY

Does how well students do at school affect how they feel? Or does how they feel affect how well they do? Or is it both? Eager to answer these questions, researchers from Germany, England, Australia and Japan tracked over 2,000 teenage students from 42 schools for five years to find out.

THE MAIN FINDINGS

1 The relationship between positive emotions and grades work both ways. The more students **enjoyed maths and took pride** in their work, the **higher** their grades were. Likewise, the **more success** that students had, the more **pride and enjoyment** they felt.

2 The **more negative** emotions that students experienced, the **worse their grades** were. These included:

- ✔ **Anger**
- ✔ **Anxiety**
- ✔ **Shame**
- ✔ **Boredom**
- ✔ **Hopelessness**

3 The most powerful **predictor of negative grades** was the amount of anxiety and hopelessness that students felt. Again, this **worked both ways**, with consistent failure increasing the intensity of these negative emotions.

4 The researchers also found that **girls reported lower** enjoyment, lower pride, more boredom, higher anxiety, more shame and more hopelessness in maths classes than boys.

Ref: Pekrun et al, 2017, *Child Development*

THE ONE ABOUT EMOTIONS AND ACHIEVEMENT

 ## RELATED RESEARCH

The finding from this study that emotions and achievement have a reciprocal relationship (i.e., that it works both ways) supports previous research in this area. For example, several studies have found that students who experience test anxiety are more likely to perform worse, which in turn makes them more likely to experience more test anxiety. That is, a negative feedback loop exists.

It is interesting that this study focused on emotional reactions towards maths, as this is consistently one of the subjects that students report having very strong feelings about. Female students regularly report less enjoyment and more anxiety in maths than boys do, even when they achieve similar results. This difference is not down to biological variation but to a combination of the different type of praise boys and girls receive and their attributions for the causes of their failures (#17, #39).

PARENTING IMPLICATIONS

The findings from this study suggest that parents should take a two-pronged approach when helping children. The first is to help them manage and nurture their emotions so that they can get better grades. The second is to develop their abilities and knowledge so that they will experience better emotions. By only focusing on one aspect, such as improving their well-being or just improving their maths expertise, we miss an opportunity to help them develop. A combination of the two is required.

The authors of this study state that their findings "suggest that educators, administrators and parents alike should consider intensifying efforts that strengthen adolescents' positive emotions and minimize their negative emotions". They suggest that this can be done by "providing students with opportunities to experience success (e.g., using intrapersonal standards to evaluate achievement; emphasising mastery over competition goals) may help to promote positive emotions and prevent negative emotions".

THE ONE ABOUT INTERACTING WITH NATURE

@inner_drive | www.innerdrive.co.uk

THE STUDY

Researchers from the University of Michigan ran two experiments to find out if interacting with nature during a study break improved students' feelings, concentration and memory.

To test this, they first looked at whether where you go for a walk has an effect. In a second study, students spent their study break either looking at photos of nature or of busy city centres. The researchers then compared the two groups.

THE MAIN FINDINGS

In the first study, students took their study break by going for a 50-minute walk either in a park or in a busy urban area. The researchers found that:

1 Students who took a break by going for a **walk in nature improved** their performance on an attention and memory task by **16**%. Students who went for a walk in an **urban environment did not improve** their scores.

2 Walking outside in the park **helped students all year round**. The season or weather made no difference.

3 Furthermore, those who walked in nature had a **positive boost** in their mood afterwards. Those who walked in urban environments didn't.

In the second study, they found that students who looked at photos of nature:

✔ **Performed better on memory and attention tests**

✔ **Had improved executive functioning**

✔ **Felt better and more refreshed afterwards**

Ref: Berman et al, 2008, *Psychological Science*

THE ONE ABOUT INTERACTING WITH NATURE

 ## RELATED RESEARCH

A recent study (#42) found that people who went on a short walk, even for just 5 minutes, had an increase in happiness, attentiveness and confidence. The participants in the study had the positive benefit of their walk regardless of whether they did it outside, in a gallery or on a treadmill.

This suggests that a walking break doesn't necessarily have to be done somewhere soothing, just that it shouldn't be somewhere stressful. As the authors of this study note, "unlike natural environments, urban environments are filled with stimulation that captures attention dramatically and additionally requires directed attention (e.g., to avoid being hit by a car), making them less restorative".

As well as walking, other research has studied simple day-to-day activities people can do to enhance memory, attention and well-being. These include getting a regular night's sleep (#24, #72), eating breakfast (#30) and drinking plenty of water. None of these strategies are particularly sophisticated or complicated. Perhaps that is the beauty of them: they have almost no cost, are easy to understand and can be put into action immediately. Furthermore, they lead to tangible and meaningful change almost instantly.

PARENTING IMPLICATIONS

The authors of this study start their write-up with a thought experiment: "Imagine a therapy that had no known side effects, was readily available and could improve your cognitive functioning at zero cost". Their results suggest that interacting with nature, be it either a walk or looking at photos, does exactly this.

Students are often encouraged to take some breaks over the course of the day whilst they are revising. The results from this study suggest that not all breaks are equal. Doing so in a way that requires one's brain to be alert is unlikely to have the desired effects. If we teach children about the advantages of taking a break in a manner that is both relaxing and refreshing, then they are more likely to not only feel better afterwards, but they are also more likely to remember more of their subsequent revision sessions.

THE ONE ABOUT STRESS AND UNCERTAINTY

@inner_drive | www.innerdrive.co.uk

THE STUDY

Researchers from University College London ran an experiment in which participants completed a learning game and received mild electric shocks that were delivered with varying predictability in order to stress them out.

The researchers wanted to find out **a)** what was the link between the feelings of uncertainty and of stress and **b)** if the two were linked, then what impact would there be on performance?

THE MAIN FINDINGS

1 Uncertainty is a **major cause** of how stressed people feel. This suggests that it is not the worst-case scenario that makes people really stressed, it is **the ambiguity of not knowing**.

2 Uncertainty **triggers** the major physiological **signatures of stress**, such as an increase in cortisol (the "stress hormone"), wider pupils and sweaty hands.

3 Some stress and uncertainty is actually **a good thing**, with participants in this condition doing better. This may be because it prompted them to **focus more and work harder**.

Ref: De Berker et al, 2016, *Nature Communications*

THE ONE ABOUT STRESS AND UNCERTAINTY

 ## RELATED RESEARCH

A growing body of research from both sport and education has examined the varying ways in which people approach and reflect on a potentially stressful situation (#32). If people believe they have skills and resources to meet the situation, feel in control of the event, surround themselves with supportive people and remember previous similar experiences, then they are more likely to view an event as a "challenge". Whereas those who feel isolated, focus on what they stand to lose if things go wrong, are overwhelmed by nerves, worry about looking bad and feel that their goals are unobtainable, are more likely to be in a "threat state". People who view events as a challenge instead of a threat are more likely to manage their stress levels effectively.

In line with this thinking, a separate study found that someone's "stress mindset" can have a significant impact on their performance (#43). Those who accepted that stress can sometimes be helpful were more likely to feel better, perform to a higher level and seek out more feedback during stressful situations. Furthermore, this stress mindset is malleable, meaning that people who learn about the potential benefits of stress can go on to cope with it more effectively.

PARENTING IMPLICATIONS

Certain situations are known to be more stressful for many children. These include exams, deadlines, public speaking and interviews. These events are considered stressful because they all have an element of uncertainty. The outcome is unsure, and the consequences of both success and failure can have a significant impact on the lives of students and their future choices.

The findings from this study offer several practical suggestions for students. Firstly, understanding the triggers of stress (i.e., uncertainty) can help improve self-awareness of why students feel the way they are. Secondly, the knowledge that uncertainty, and indeed stress, can help enhance performance should be reassuring and can help normalise these feelings. Thirdly, if children feel that their stress levels are excessively high and want to reduce them, then gathering information with the aim of reducing ambiguity and uncertainty will help.

THE ONE ABOUT METACOGNITION

@inner_drive | www.innerdrive.co.uk

THE STUDY

Metacognition refers to students' ability to monitor and direct their own learning effectively. It is seen as an essential part of developing independent learners. As such, it is a growing interest for researchers and teachers alike.

Researchers recently tested if improving student metacognition, by having them answer simple study skills questions, would improve their academic achievements. They compared these students with a control group, and then monitored how all the students studied for and performed during their exams.

THE MAIN FINDINGS

1 To **improve their metacognition**, students should reflect on **three questions**:
- Which resources do I need to help me study?
- Why are those resources helpful?
- How will I use this resource?

2 Asking these questions improved students' **self-reflection** and how **effective** they found their study resources when learning. They also felt **less stressed** and **more in control**.

3 These students went on to score **a third of a grade higher** in their classes. They also did better on each exam. This was true for **all students**, regardless of their gender, age or academic ability.

Ref: Chen et al, 2017, *Psychological Science*

THE ONE ABOUT METACOGNITION

 ## RELATED RESEARCH

A growing body of evidence suggests developing students' metacognitive skills leads to a boost in their motivation, learning and exam results. Several studies have found that it is not just the quantity of studying they do, but also the quality as well. Students who can effectively and efficiently use and manage the resources made available to them are the ones who tend to go on to achieve higher academic success.

Researchers from the Education Endowment Foundation in England suggest that this can add up to seven months of additional progress if implemented effectively. Encouragingly, several studies have found that metacognition is something that can be taught, learnt and developed. One such study found positive gains within two weeks of helping their students improve their metacognition.

Other studies have found that many students typically struggle to bridge the gap from having good intentions to actual behaviour change (#6). However, evidence suggests that those who do come up with specific action plans (as was the case in this study) often manage to do this better.

PARENTING IMPLICATIONS

Many parents pay a lot of money to provide high quality study resources for their children. However, the authors of this study note that:

> Regardless of how richly we endow students with study materials, support and environments conducive to learning, many of these resources will be wasted on students who do not thoughtfully use them in a productive manner. Encouraging students to be strategic in their use of class resources to master the class material enables them to leverage more of their potential during performance.

The researchers end their study on a positive note, reflecting on the long-term benefit that children will gain from developing their metacognitive abilities. They note that:

> "Beyond education, there are many other situations in real life in which people engage in goal pursuit ineffectively . . . encouraging self-reflection in people about how to approach their goals strategically with the resources that are available to them can go a long way in helping them achieve their goals. This suggests that our students will continue to reap the rewards of improving metacognition long after their time in school has finished".

THE ONE ABOUT PICTURING THE PROCESS

@inner_drive | www.innerdrive.co.uk

THE STUDY

It is one week before an exam. Is it better to visualise yourself studying for the exam or is it better to visualise what life would be like if you did well in the exam? Researchers ran a study with 101 students to find out.

In this study, some of the students were instructed to picture themselves revising, whereas others were told to imagine finding out that they had achieved a high grade on the test. The researchers then recorded how the students felt in the build-up to the exam, how much revision they did and finally, what grade they got.

THE MAIN FINDINGS

1 One week before the exam, students who spent **just a few minutes visualising themselves studying**, instead of seeing themselves doing well in the test, reported that they:

✔ **Had a clearer plan of what they needed to do**

✔ **Felt less nervous about the exam**

✔ **Were going to spend more time studying**

✔ **Expected to do better in the exam**

2 The day after the exam, the researchers found out that students **who had visualised themselves studying** instead of **doing well in the test**:

✔ **Did 40% more revision in the final week**

✔ **Got over 8% higher marks in their exam**

✔ **Outperformed the class average by some distance, whereas those who visualised their desired outcome did worse**

Ref: Pham and Taylor, 1999, *Personality and Social Psychology Bulletin*

THE ONE ABOUT PICTURING THE PROCESS

RELATED RESEARCH

Previous research on visualisation has found that it can be particularly helpful in enhancing emotions, which in turn are linked with academic success (#49). However - and in support of this study - other research has found a darker side to visualisation. A rather fascinating and quirky study found that, for participants who were trying to lose weight, after visualising the outcome - such as the amount of weight they wanted to lose - participants were more likely to be tempted by the offer of free doughnuts. Focusing too much on the outcome can have a detrimental effect.

Within education, other studies have found that students who spent time imagining that their week was going to be great actually reported being less energised and achieved less over the seven days than those in a control group. Likewise, similar results were found in students who spent time visualising their perfect job. Upon graduation, these students received fewer job offers and had a lower starting wage than those who did not do this type of visualisation.

PARENTING IMPLICATIONS

This study gives an indication of how we can best help children both prepare for upcoming exams and manage their emotions whilst doing so. Helping them focus on the behaviours they need to have to succeed will ensure that they are more likely to complete the right actions. Focusing too much on the outcome may further exacerbate procrastination and daydreaming, as well as enhancing anxiety about the exam by focusing too much on the destination and not on the journey itself. Essentially, as the authors state, "a student who wishes to become a surgeon would improve his or her chances by mentally stimulating the steps he or she must go through to achieve that goal rather than envisioning him or herself in the desired end state".

The authors of the study conclude with a famous, albeit anonymous, quote: "The will to win is not nearly as important as the will to prepare to win". They state that instead of having an "I can do it" attitude, students would be better placed having a "how can I do it?" one instead.

THE ONE ABOUT PARENTAL WARMTH

@inner_drive | www.innerdrive.co.uk

THE STUDY

Researchers recently investigated how much the type and frequency of communication that parents have with their children impacts their child's development. To find out, they tracked 565 children and their parents over a two-year period. During that time, both parents and children were regularly surveyed to find out how the parents felt they communicated with their children, how the children perceived this communication and what the consequences of it were.

The researchers specifically looked at parental over-praising ("my child is more special than other children"), parental warmth ("I let my child know I love them"), the children's self-esteem ("kids like me are happy with themselves as a person") and narcissism ("kids like me deserve something extra").

THE MAIN FINDINGS

1 The **consequences** of parents **over-praising** included:

- **Children displaying more narcissistic behaviours**

- **No difference in their child's self-esteem levels**

2 Parental warmth led to:

- **Children having higher levels of self-esteem**

- **Did not make the children more narcissistic**

They concluded that "parent-training interventions might be one effective means to curtail narcissistic development. Such interventions can help parents convey affection and appreciation to children without conveying to children that they are superior to others".

Ref: Brummelman et al, 2015, *Proceedings of the National Academy of Sciences*

THE ONE ABOUT PARENTAL WARMTH

 ## RELATED RESEARCH

The area of narcissism has fascinated people ever since the mythological Greek figure Narcissus exclaimed that "the spark I kindle is the torch I carry". Researchers have distinguished narcissism from self-esteem by describing the former as "passionately wanting to think well of oneself" and the latter as actually "thinking well of oneself". Self-esteem has been associated with lower levels of anxiety and depression, whereas narcissism has been associated with stress, feelings of humiliation and a range of mental health problems.

In the quest to promote high self-esteem in children, many parents were previously advised to lavishly praise them to reinforce all the good things they were doing. Unfortunately, not only has lavish praise been found to be associated with lowering expectations, but this study suggests that it does not boost self-esteem; in fact, that it drives the exact type of narcissistic behaviours we want to avoid.

Likewise, other evidence (#17) suggests that the type of praise children hear when they are as young as 1 year old can predict their mindset up to five years later, with those that receive comments about their natural abilities and achievements being more likely to develop a fixed mindset compared to those who had heard praise about their behaviour, effort and strategy.

PARENTING IMPLICATIONS

The authors of the study note that "children come to see themselves as they believe to be seen by significant others, as if they learn to see themselves through other eyes" and

> When children are seen by their parents as being more special and more entitled than other children, they may internalize the view that they are superior individuals, a view that is at the core of narcissism. However, when children are treated by their parents with affection and appreciation, they may internalize the view that they are valuable individuals, a view that is at the core of self-esteem.

This provides food for thought – in the rush to help develop their self-confidence we run the risk of using a sledgehammer to crack a nut. Positive but honest and accurate feedback and praise offers a better solution.

THE ONE ABOUT HOW MUCH WE FORGET

@inner_drive | www.innerdrive.co.uk

THE STUDY

In 1880, German psychologist Hermann Ebbinghaus conducted one of the most famous studies ever. He wanted to see how quickly people forget things over time. He was the first to try to find a mathematical equation that describes that shape of forgetting. The result, called "the forgetting curve", is often presented something like this:

Ebbinghaus Forgetting Curve

RETENTION

100%
80%
60%
40%
20%
0%

100%
58%
44%
36%
33%
28%
25%
21%

IMMEDIATELY   20 MINUTES   1 HOUR   9 HOURS   1 DAY   2 DAYS   6 DAYS   31 DAYS

ELAPSED TIME SINCE LEARNING

Over 130 years later, researchers from The University of Amsterdam sought to replicate and update his findings using modern statistical analysis and experimental procedures.

THE MAIN FINDINGS

1 Generally speaking, Ebbinghaus' findings were replicated – people suffer **a drop in memory soon after the event**, with this decline then slowing down over time.

2 However, they found that people receive **a boost to memory** after 24 hours, with their participants remembering **more in the morning** of the second day than they did in the night of the first. This jump is due to the negative impact fatigue has on memory and the power that sleep has to combat this.

3 People tend to remember **the first** and the **last things** they learn more than the things in the middle. These are called the **primacy and recency effects**, respectively.

4 The researchers advised that "the forgetting curve" is **not set in stone**. Instead, it is better to see it as **a guide**.

Ref: Murre and Dros, 2015, *PLoS ONE*

THE ONE ABOUT HOW MUCH WE FORGET

 ## RELATED RESEARCH

A growing number of studies in cognitive, educational and developmental psychology have struggled to have their initial findings replicated. That is what makes studies like this so valuable. The authors of the study conclude with praise for Ebbinghaus by saying that he

> Set new standards for psychology experiments, already incorporating such 'modern' concepts as controlled stimulus, counter-balancing of time of day effects, guarding against optional stopping, statistical data analysis and modelling to find a concise mathematical description and further verify his results. The result was a high-quality forgetting curve that has rightfully remained a classic in the field. Replications, including ours, testify to the soundness of his results.

In the past few decades, researchers have built on this classic study by examining the amount of information that students forget over the summer holidays (#73) and the role of "spacing out learning" (#4). They have found consistently that people do forget information quickly, especially if parts of that information is taught close to one another and not returned to again.

PARENTING IMPLICATIONS

This area of study has powerful implications for how our children learn. With modular exams becoming increasingly rare in the UK, the challenge now is how children can best learn a large amount of material over the course of two years without forgetting it.

Since people often forget information quickly, it is important to encourage our children to regularly revisit old topics, especially when they are studying at home. It is this very act of forgetting and re-learning that actually cements knowledge into our long-term memory. Essentially, doing one hour a day for seven days is more effective than doing seven hours in one day; the latter will fall short because of the nature of Ebbinghaus' forgetting curve.

This means we should not assume that what was once learnt is still remembered. Our children may naturally fall into that trap about their own knowledge, so have consistently spaced-out conversations about previous topics should help ensure they retain previously learnt material.

THE ONE ABOUT MINDSET, ATTITUDE AND SELF-ESTEEM

@inner_drive | www.innerdrive.co.uk

THE STUDY

Previous research has found that when performing an experiment in a laboratory, students who feel that they have a growth mindset (i.e., the belief they can improve) think more productively and perform better in subsequent tasks than those who have a fixed mindset (i.e., the belief that their ability is set in stone). But does this translate into the real world?

Researchers tracked over 500 students over the course of their four years at University to find out if having a growth or fixed mindset impacted how they thought, felt and behaved. This included how they explained their successes, failures and changes to their self-esteem.

THE MAIN FINDINGS

1 Those with a growth mindset were more likely to:

▶ **Prioritise learning goals over performance ones**

▶ **Attribute their success to their efforts and study skills**

▶ **Feel excited, inspired and enthusiastic about their academic performance**

▶ **Put in more effort or learn from their mistakes in the face of adversity**

▶ **Have an increase in self-esteem during late adolescence**

2 Those with a fixed mindset were more likely to:

▶ **Prioritise immediate performance over learning**

▶ **Attribute both their failures and successes to external and uncontrollable factors, such as luck**

▶ **Feel distressed, ashamed and upset about their academic performance**

▶ **Give up and feel helpless in the face of adversity**

▶ **Suffer a dip in self-esteem during late adolescence**

Ref: Robins and Pals, 2002, *Self and Identity*

THE ONE ABOUT MINDSET, ATTITUDE AND SELF-ESTEEM

RELATED RESEARCH

This research supports and builds on previous findings that highlight the different behaviours and thought processes of those with a growth or fixed mindset. It is encouraging to see research moving beyond the laboratory and being tested in real-world situations.

One interesting area of study has found that helping students realise that their personality is not fixed has helped reduce anxiety and depression symptoms. Likewise, helping students adapt their mindset towards stress – that is, helping them realise that stress is not always a bad thing – has helped improve student performance in the face of adversity (#43).

The finding in this study – that those with a growth mindset are more likely to adopt learning instead of performance goals – is interesting. Other research (#5) has found that those who adopt a learning orientation are more likely to spend longer on the task, work harder, display more resilience, choose challenging tasks and have more pride and satisfaction in their work.

PARENTING IMPLICATIONS

This study highlights that how students view themselves can impact how they explain their successes and failures, self-esteem and indeed future goals. Beyond just academic grades, it suggests that the growth mindset theory can fundamentally shape how students view their educational experience and alters their perception of how much control they have over it.

The researchers state that those with a fixed mindset:

> Explain academic achievement – both successes and failures – in terms of external factors . . . thus they are truly helpless and assume that both their successes and failures are out of their control. In a sense, they are caught in a trap: they strive for academic success to prove their high ability, yet they explain away their successes as due to luck.

Whereas those with a growth mindset "believe they just need to try harder or use better study strategies to perform better". Helping guide our children towards having a growth mindset offers a promising strategy to help them better navigate their school life.

THE ONE ABOUT LEARNING STYLES

@inner_drive | www.innerdrive.co.uk

THE STUDY

The learning style theory states that we each have a "learning style" such as "visual", "auditory" or "kinaesthetic". Further, pupils who are taught in a way that complements their "learning style" will learn and perform better. But is there any evidence to back up this theory?

Four professors of psychology in the US performed a thorough review of all the research available to see if the claims made by proponents of the learning style theory stacked up.

THE MAIN FINDINGS

1 **Preferences, not styles:** Students may have a preference for the way that they want to learn. However, this is not the same as having a learning style. A preference is **what you like the most,** not necessarily the way you would learn best.

2 **Absence of positive findings:** The researchers could not find a single study where teaching someone in their "learning style" led to them getting better results.

3 **Evidence of negative findings:** There is, however, a significant amount of evidence that students who were taught in their favourite style did no better. This was found to be true in a wide range of settings, including education, medicine and in psychology laboratories.

4 **Decide how to teach the content based on what is being taught**. For example, the researchers noted that "the optimal curriculum for a writing course probably includes a heavy verbal emphasis, whereas the most efficient and effective model of teaching geometry obviously requires visual-spatial materials".

5 Even **if research found a positive impact** of teaching students according to their styles (which it hasn't), the impact **would have to be very large** to justify the time, energy and cost of doing it.

Ref: Pashler et al, 2008, *Psychological Science in the Public Interest*

THE ONE ABOUT LEARNING STYLES

RELATED RESEARCH

A survey in 2012 found that the learning style myth is still prevalent in the UK: 93% of people believe it. It is quite difficult to discuss the related research in this area as it is marked by a notable absence of any research into the efficacy of the application of the "learning styles theory". This was the core finding of this research paper.

However, one other study is worth noting, which found that having students use a range and combination of senses whilst they learn something new will often lead to better performances as it will help keep their attention and will also help embed the content more in their long-term memory. This suggests that not only is just teaching someone to their learning style less effective but also that it can actually limit how much students learn.

PARENTING IMPLICATIONS

Why have learning styles become so popular? Apart from the desire to categorise people, the authors of the study note that

> If a person or person's child is not succeeding or excelling school, it may be more comfortable for the person to think that the educational system, not the person or the child himself or herself, is responsible. That is, rather than attribute one's lack of success to any lack of ability or effort on one's part, it may be more appealing to think that the fault lies with instruction being inadequately tailored to one's learning style.

This uncomfortable truth lays the foundation for much more positive growth. By focusing more on the things that matter; motivation (#40), work ethic (#18), attitude and effective learning strategies (#1), parents can focus on the behaviours that will best help their child succeed. Using bogus reasons such as learning styles to explain a child's failure may make us feel better in the short term, as it externalises the cause of the failure. However, in the long term, it pigeonholes the child and stops us from focusing on strategies that will actually lead to that child's growth.

THE ONE ABOUT EATING DINNER TOGETHER

THE STUDY

@inner_drive | www.innerdrive.co.uk

Families are now far less likely to eat meals together regularly than they were in the past. But what impact does regular family meal times have on student development? To find out, researchers surveyed almost 100,000 students from over 213 cities.

THE MAIN FINDINGS

1 More than half of young teenagers ate dinner with their family 5–7 times a week. This number **dropped to just over a third** for older teenagers.

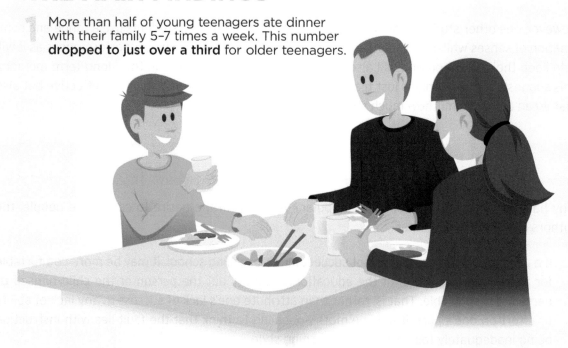

2 Children who regularly ate dinner with their family **reported enhanced**:

- ✓ **Communication with their parents**
- ✓ **Parental involvement in school**
- ✓ **Motivation levels**
- ✓ **School engagement and time spent on homework**
- ✓ **Self-esteem**
- ✓ **Ability to plan and make decisions**
- ✓ **Optimism about their future**

3 Children who regularly ate dinner with their family **reported less**:

- ✓ **Alcohol use**
- ✓ **Tobacco use**
- ✓ **Drug use**
- ✓ **Depressive symptoms**
- ✓ **Anti-social behaviour**
- ✓ **Violent tendencies**
- ✓ **Problems at school**

Ref: Fulker et al, 2006, *Journal of Adolescent Health*

THE ONE ABOUT EATING DINNER TOGETHER

 ## RELATED RESEARCH

Other research has focused not only on frequency of family mealtimes but on what families do during those times. One such study found that one-third of children report watching television whilst eating with their parents. This was associated with eating fewer vegetables, drinking more fizzy drinks and consuming higher amounts of fats. However, it is worth noting that these children still had a healthier diet than those who did not eat regularly with their family.

Eating dinner as a family has also been shown to help teenagers create dietary habits that stick with them into adulthood. This aligns with other research that found similar effects for eating breakfast regularly as a child (#30). Evidence suggests that the effects of both have decreased over the past 30 years, but that by planning what to eat and scheduling time to do so together, families could change this.

PARENTING IMPLICATIONS

Although this study looked at correlations and not causation, the authors do suggest that "adolescents may learn social skills and develop a more positive self-worth during mealtime interactions". Therefore, although not proven in this study itself, it is not unreasonable to suggest that eating together has many positive consequences.

This raises two interesting thoughts. Firstly, as well as offering the opportunity for parents to monitor the quality of what their children eat, family mealtimes have the added bonus of facilitating lots of little conversations with them. This means that potential worries, stresses and anxieties can be nipped in the bud before they become full-blown crises. This means it can be a very subtle yet effective route to opening conversation pathways with our children.

Secondly, how can we best do this when we live busy lives when having to work late hours or do shift work? The truth is there is no easy or answer or handy work-around. Eating together makes such a big difference, which means even if it is not possible all the time, we do prioritise doing it some of the time. Doing so will have a significant impact in boosting both your child's character and their academic performance.

THE ONE ABOUT ELECTRONIC NOTE-TAKING

@inner_drive | www.innerdrive.co.uk

THE STUDY

Technology is playing an ever-increasing role in education. It is now common to see students taking notes using electronic devices, be it laptops or tablets. But which is better for note-taking: pen and paper, or electronics?

Researchers investigated how students differed in the type of notes they took depending on the device they used, how well they could subsequently apply the knowledge learnt during their lesson and how well they did on their final exams.

THE MAIN FINDINGS

1 Those who took notes with a laptop **performed worse** when they had to answer conceptual-application questions.

2 Those who took notes on their laptops wrote up to **30% more words** than those who did so on paper. They were also more likely to take notes verbatim. Taking notes verbatim **leads to shallower learning** as it does not require the student to think about what they are typing.

3 Even if the lecturers told students about **the cost** of taking notes down word for word on the laptop, this had no impact. They **still did** so.

4 Students were given the chance to review their notes before the final exam. Those **who took notes using pen and paper outperformed** those who took notes on their laptop.

Ref: Mueller and Oppenheimer, 2014, *Psychological Science*

THE ONE ABOUT ELECTRONIC NOTE-TAKING

 ## RELATED RESEARCH

A recent study has failed to replicate some of the findings in this study. However, the jury is still out, and it is worth noting that several other studies have found that students who take notes on laptops struggle to stay on task, since they succumb to the numerous online temptations such as streaming videos, social networking and shopping.

The type of notes that students take with their laptops makes a difference. Students are more likely to take notes verbatim, since they can type faster than they can write. However, several studies have confirmed that doing so leads to less cognitive processing and, because of this, less information is retained. The researchers of this study offer another suggestion as to why students who took notes by hand performed better, commenting that since they had to go slower, students were forced to select "more important information to include in their notes, which enables them to study the content more efficiently".

PARENTING IMPLICATIONS

The authors conclude with a clear word of warning over the use of laptops for note-taking when they say that "laptop use can negatively affect performance on educational assessments, even - or perhaps especially - when they computer is used for its intended function of easier note taking". Essentially, parents should be aware that technology may not provide the quick and neat solutions that they are hoping for. Instead, they should encourage their children to think about how they take notes in class, because as the authors say, there is real value in having "desirable difficulty".

This is not to say that laptops can't provide some unique learning opportunities, such as access to wider information quickly, but there is an opportunity cost. The best way to view laptops is with "a healthy dose of caution; despite their growing popularity, laptops may be doing more harm in classrooms than good". In the rush to embrace technology and give our children every opportunity to learn, we should be cautious and careful in doing so.

THE ONE ABOUT THE BANDWAGON EFFECT

@inner_drive | www.innerdrive.co.uk

THE STUDY

Do students know their own mind or are they likely to follow the crowd? What if they think the crowd is doing the wrong thing, will they still go along with them? This is known as the Bandwagon Effect, which describes the likelihood of people of doing something because everyone else is.

Groups of students were asked to publicly state how long they thought a line was. Unbeknownst to the real participant, everyone else in the room was an actor and were all under instructions to give false answers. Would the real participant give the correct answer or follow the group and get it wrong?

THE MAIN FINDINGS

1. In about a **third of the experiments**, participants **followed the group** and gave a wrong answer.

2. When in the presence of others, **75% gave a wrong answer** at least once.

3. When they were **on their own**, people stated the **correct answer** more than **99%** of the time.

4. In interviews afterwards, **participants who followed the group** and got it wrong said they did so either because of **low** confidence, they thought the group knew best, or that they suspected everyone else was wrong but had a desire to conform and fit in.

Ref: Asch, 1951, Groups, *Leadership and Men*

THE ONE ABOUT THE BANDWAGON EFFECT

 ## RELATED RESEARCH

Following on from his original research, Solomon Asch investigated under which conditions people are most likely to conform. He found that the number of other people stating the wrong answer had an impact: only one person stating a false answer led to an error rate of 3%, two people stating a false answer increased this to 13% and three people stating a false answer resulted in an error rate of 32%. Increasing the number of people giving false statements beyond three did not appear to alter conformity levels.

More recent studies have found that the bandwagon effect occurs in situations beyond the psych lab. For example, one such study found that hotel guests were more likely to reuse their towels (and thus save the hotel laundry costs) if they believed that the other guests in the hotel were also doing so.

The impact that other people have on decision making has been extensively studied in adolescents. It is interesting to note how most risky decisions - that is, smoking, underage drinking and speeding whilst driving - happen in the presence of others. This suggests that we are all prone to the Bandwagon Effect, but also that teenagers are especially so (#7).

PARENTING IMPLICATIONS

This line of research has interesting implications for parents on two separate levels. First, is that it is easy to get into a state of "group-think", which is when people fail to critically evaluate the quality of a suggestion because many other people say it is good. This is evident when people parent in a style that they see other parents doing, as opposed to backing their own judgement.

Secondly, the Bandwagon Effect explains why students may think and behave differently when part of a group than they do when they are on their own. In this study, some participants reported knowing that the answer they were giving was wrong but that they did so anyway because of social pressure. Helping your child know their own mind and to not make bad decisions "just because everyone else is" may prove to be one of the more valuable skills needed to navigate the tricky teenage years.

THE ONE ABOUT RETRIEVAL PRACTICE AND STRESS

@inner_drive | www.innerdrive.co.uk

THE STUDY

Are students who revise using retrieval practice better able to recall that information when they are stressed, such as in highly pressurised exams? To find out, researchers had half their students revise by doing lots of tests and quizzes (i.e., retrieval practice) and the other half revise by re-reading key passages of the text. They then placed half of each group in either stressful or non-stressful environments and recorded how much they were able to remember.

THE MAIN FINDINGS

1 Those who revised **using retrieval practice outperformed** those who had just re-read their notes by **17-26%**

2 Increased stress made those who **studied by re-reading** their notes perform up to **32% worse.**

3 Increased stress **did not negatively affect** the memory of those who used **retrieval practice**.

4 Retrieval practice **was so effective** at combating the negative effect of stress on memory that the stressed retrieval practice **students performed better** than those who weren't stressed and had used the re-reading technique for their revision.

Ref: Smith et al, 2016, *Science*

THE ONE ABOUT RETRIEVAL PRACTICE AND STRESS

RELATED RESEARCH

Stress has been found to impair memory because of an increase in cortisol released in the brain. This blocks the pathways near the hippocampus (the part of the brain largely responsible for memory), making it harder to recall things. Retrieval practice offers a way around this, as the act of having to generate an answer creates numerous and clear routes to access the information in our brain, essentially circumventing the stress blockade.

It is interesting to note that stress levels seem to be contagious, with two separate studies finding that parental stress level is often transferred to their child, as are teacher stress levels to their students. There is some evidence however to suggest that stress is not always a bad thing (#43). Too little stress and people can feel lethargic and full of apathy. However, too much stress can lead to a reduction in memory because of excessive anxiety and narrowing focus. It therefore appears that there is a Goldilocks level when it comes to stress, with just the right amount aiding performance.

PARENTING IMPLICATIONS

This study suggests that by teaching students the importance of retrieval, be it quizzes, essay answers, verbally answering a question or multiple-choice tests, we can not only help them learn the content at a faster rate, we can also help ensure that they can access this knowledge when they are under stress in their final exams.

The message to children couldn't be clearer or simpler: don't study in order to do well at the test. Do lots of tests in order to study well. By doing so, they will learn more and perform better under pressure. This means they will be able to deliver their best when it matters the most.

THE ONE ABOUT FALSE CONFIDENCE

@inner_drive | www.innerdrive.co.uk

THE STUDY

Researchers tested whether watching someone else perform a task gives an inaccurate and over-inflated sense of confidence that you can do it as well. They ran a series of studies that had participants watch other people successfully perform a range of tasks. These included doing the tablecloth trick, moonwalking, playing darts and online video gaming. They then measured how confident the participants were at doing it themselves and then had them perform the task to assess the accuracy of their confidence.

THE MAIN FINDINGS

1 The more that people **watch someone else do a skill**, the more likely they are to believe **they can do it** as well.

2 **More doesn't always equal better.** Watching someone else many times did not improve actual ability relative to watching it once.

3 Interestingly, when people had to read about a task, or think about doing it, it **didn't increase their confidence**.

This increase in self-belief only occurred when watching someone else do it.

4 **This false confidence** from watching someone else many times comes from knowing "**what steps to take** but not how those **steps feel** when taking them".

Ref: Kardas and O'Brien, 2018, *Psychological Science*

THE ONE ABOUT FALSE CONFIDENCE

 RELATED RESEARCH

Other evidence suggests that even watching a skilled performer from multiple angles and in slow motion is not enough to master a skill from sight alone, since "no matter how many times people watch a performance, they never gain one critical piece: the feeling of doing". Research does suggest that observing others is better than doing nothing, but to really develop talents and expertise requires many hours of deliberate practice.

A recent survey asked students which of the following options would they seek first and then use most to help them learn new material. The options were a) watching others perform the task, b) reading about it or c) hearing the instructions. Overall, watching others perform was reported as the go-to strategy, the easiest to process and the most effective. The results from this study suggest that this may not be a wise choice. As the researchers of the study conclude, "while people may feel they are acquiring the skills that athletes, artists and technicians perform in front of their eyes, often these skills may be easier seen than done".

PARENTING IMPLICATIONS

Previous research has indicated often, the students who struggle the most are more likely to have a false sense of confidence. This is referred to as the Dunning–Kruger Effect (#16). This may be compounded by watching someone else perform a task successfully many times, as it results in a "misunderstanding of the kind and amount of practice needed during subsequent training and therefore being no better prepared".

This suggests that false confidence is the result of knowing the step-by-step guide of what to do, but not having first-hand experience of actually doing it. The former breeds confidence, whereas the latter develops competence. Therefore, it is advisable that showing children what to do may be a good start, but for learning to be truly effective, they really need to practice it for themselves.

THE ONE ABOUT READING AND BACKGROUND NOISE

@inner_drive | www.innerdrive.co.uk

THE STUDY

One of the most popular revision strategies for students is to read and re-read their notes. A wealth of research over many years has highlighted that this is likely to be a fairly ineffective technique. But if students are going to read their notes, is there a way that can help them do so in the best way? To find out, researchers conducted one of the largest literature reviews, covering 65 different studies on the topic.

THE MAIN FINDINGS

1 Background speech, noise and music all had a **negative effect** on reading comprehension. This was true **for both children and adults**.

2 **Music** – the researchers found that "there was a **95% probability** that lyrical music was **more distracting** than nonlyrical music".

3 Both background speech and music were **the biggest distraction** and are likely to be **just as distracting as each other**.

The researchers comment that **this is surprising** because "most people perceive lyrical music to be subjectively less distracting than intelligible speech".

Ref: Vasilev et al, 2018, Association for Psychological Science.

THE ONE ABOUT READING AND BACKGROUND NOISE

 ## RELATED RESEARCH

This study provides valuable insights because, despite being one of the most popular ways for students to revise for their exams, simply re-reading notes is one of the least effective strategies (#1). Other research has highlighted how, if students are going to use reading as their primary source of learning, then they should read their notes out loud (#29). The finding that we should try to minimise background noise to aid reading comprehension, as it essentially competes for our attention, is supported by other research which found that listening to music that has lyrics whilst studying also has a detrimental effect on exam results (#15).

That being said, reading is not done for the sole purpose of improving academic performance. Reading for pleasure has been associated with vocabulary development, greater exposure to a wider range of words, improved mental health, a better night's sleep and reduced decline of mental capacities in later life. Key to this is that our attitude towards reading for pleasure is heavily influenced in our formative years, which means that both schools and parents play a very important role in shaping this (#46).

PARENTING IMPLICATIONS

Studies like these are highly valuable, since a lot of independent study time is spent reading. The researchers could not be clearer when they conclude their study by saying that their results "showed that background noise, speech and music are almost always distracting, even if the distraction effects are small in size". Given that several studies have found that more than 50% of students reported studying or doing homework with music in the background; these results could help alter their learning habits for the better.

Central to achieving this change would be following a three-step programme. Firstly, students should be encouraged to self-reflect on their current study habits to see if they are making avoidable errors. Secondly, we should help educate children on the potential costs of reading and revising in environments that have excessive background noise. Finally, anything we can do to help support students by minimising background noise whilst they are reading should yield positive results.

THE ONE ABOUT TRANSITIONING TO SECONDARY SCHOOL

THE STUDY

@inner_drive | www.innerdrive.co.uk

The transition from primary to secondary school can be a difficult time for students. Young students have to deal with a new environment, an increase in number of teacher relationships they need to form and an increased workload. Evidence suggests that the stress may lead to an initial reduction in grades and attitudes towards school.

Researchers recently explored how best to help students manage this transition. To help reduce any assessment bias, they ran a double-blind experiment, in which the teachers implementing the intervention and the students receiving it are unaware whether they are the control group or the experimental group. The intervention included advice on how most struggle to fit in at first, how to engage in academic and social environments and confirming that support was available. The students also had to reflect on how they would deal with hypothetical situations.

THE MAIN FINDINGS

1 **Students in the intervention group reported:**

- ▸ **Higher levels of school trust**
- ▸ **Social belonging**
- ▸ **Lower levels of anxiety**

2 The intervention group went on to receive **higher grades overall**, as well as **fewer numbers of low grades** (D's and F's)

3 Students in the intervention group had on average

12% fewer absences

and **34% fewer behavioural referrals** than those in the control group.

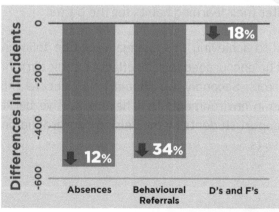

Ref: Borman et al. 2019. Proceedings of the National Academy of Sciences of the United States of America.

THE ONE ABOUT TRANSITIONING TO SECONDARY SCHOOL

 ## RELATED RESEARCH

The transition from primary school to secondary school can feel especially daunting as students at this age are already going through many physical and psychological changes. Other research suggests that this stress is magnified when joining a new school because of the increased work requirement; new, multiple teacher-student relationships; and navigating larger buildings.

Several studies have found that the stress of starting secondary school often leads to an initial reduction in grades, decline in self-esteem and negative attitude towards teachers. One study suggested a potential route to navigating these challenges. Researchers from Columbia University and Stanford University tracked teenagers over two years and found evidence to suggest that students' mindsets affected how well they managed these transitions. They found that those with a growth mindset (#5, #56) were more likely to get higher grades, take on learning goals, value effort and adopt positive coping strategies, and these students were less likely to feel helpless than students with a fixed mindset.

Transitions from one stage of education to another have also been studied in older students moving from secondary school to university. One recent study found that key to managing this change was keeping a sense of perspective, maintaining good physical health and creating/maintaining support networks.

PARENTING IMPLICATIONS

Supporting students when they transition to secondary school should start when they are still in primary school. Previous research has found that offering taster days, giving children clear information to set expectations and using some of next year's material in advance are all helpful strategies. Likewise, evidence from this study suggests that pre-empting and removing some of the taboo of their worries (which typically include how most students are concerned that they won't fit in or how to behave) will help facilitate this transition.

Using hypothetical situations that students may have to deal with offers a good chance for parents to get an insight into how their children are currently feeling. It also helps the students talk through and explore possible solutions which will help to normalise the new situation they find themselves in.

THE ONE ABOUT DRAWING FOR LEARNING

@inner_drive | www.innerdrive.co.uk

THE STUDY

The "production effect" states that if students create something new with the material they are learning from, it helps them to cement that content in their long-term memory. This has previously been studied by having students produce a lesson for other students or reading out loud (which "produces" sounds from the words, instead of reading in silence).

But what about drawing pictures of what they were learning? Would this also count as an example of the production effect? Researchers from universities in Germany and America collaborated to find out. They compared students who simply read a key text with those who read and also drew pictures of it. They also tested to see whether drawing the picture themselves, or having it given to them made a difference.

THE MAIN FINDINGS

1 Students who also drew pictures **performed significantly better** in the final tests. This was true for both their comprehension tests and when they had to replicate their drawings.

2 Students who also drew pictures **needed more learning time** (as it took them longer to produce their diagrams). However, additional analysis showed that **it was the act of drawing** and not just the additional learning time that **made them perform better**.

3 Students who also drew pictures **reported putting more effort into their learning**. This is likely to account for their improved performance.

4 Students who had to do their own drawing **performed better in subsequent tests** than those who had been given the diagram already finished.

Ref: Schmeck et al, 2014, Contemporary Educational Psychology.

THE ONE ABOUT DRAWING FOR LEARNING

 ## RELATED RESEARCH

The impact that drawing has on learning has been studied and replicated numerous times over the past 30 years. The researchers of this paper summarise these findings, explaining that

> by drawing, learners are no longer passive consumers of information and knowledge; they are actively involved in the cognitive processes of selecting, organizing and integrating the information to be learned. Thus, learner-generated drawing is a cognitive learning strategy that is aimed to foster learning from the text, and if used adequately, drawing can increase learning outcomes.

This is expanded on later when they summarised one of the seminal studies in this area by stating that there are three processes that aid this learning.

> First, learners select the relevant key information from the text. Second, the selected key information is organized to build up an internal verbal representation of the text information. Third, learners construct an internal nonverbal (visual) representation of the text information and connect it with the verbal representation and with relevant prior knowledge.

Essentially it helps them select, organise and recall information, which helps cement it in their long-term knowledge.

PARENTING IMPLICATIONS

The researchers highlight how the students were given some prompts and structure on how to create their drawings in this experiment. This suggests that doing so may provide enough of a framework for students to work from but also enough autonomy for them to have to work hard at generating the diagrams themselves. This would be something for parents to bear in mind if they are considering using this production effect for their children when they are at home studying for their exams.

One popular way that students tend to study is to create a mind-map in which themes, concepts and key points are drawn out connected to one another. However, many students often do this containing only words. This study suggests that getting students to incorporate pictures, drawings and diagrams may be an additional way to help them accelerate their learning.

THE ONE ABOUT PARENTAL INVOLVEMENT

@inner_drive | www.innerdrive.co.uk

THE STUDY

An area of research that has long interested many people is how parental involvement in a child's education can impact their academic achievements. Parental involvement can be defined and measured in several ways but is generally seen as a combination of how engaged parents are at home and with the school, and how positive their attitudes are towards their child's education, school and teachers.

One study that shed some light on this area tracked various factors on 158 primary-aged students. These included the level of parental involvement, student IQ, academic performance, perceived academic competence and teacher–student relationship. These were measured using both standardised tests and by teachers filling in questionnaires.

THE MAIN FINDINGS

1 Parental involvement was **positively associated with student's academic performance** in the classroom, over and beyond the variance accounted for by the child's IQ.

2 After **controlling for a child's IQ**, parental involvement was **positively associated** with:

✓ **Students having good relationships with their teachers.**

✓ **How students perceive their own cognitive ability.**

3 Once the student–teacher relationship was accounted for, parental involvement **did not predict** the child's academic performance. This highlights the **importance of the teacher–student relationship**.

The researchers do point out that **there are several limitations to their study**, notably that several of the measures that were being monitored, were taken based on the teacher's perception and opinion. This may have led to **some inaccuracies**, "specifically, it may be that some teachers were unduly influenced by outside factors, such as the parent being involved in the school's PTA and were unable to determine the parent's actual attitude toward the child's education".

Ref: Topor et al. 2010, Journal of Prevention & Intervention in the Community.

THE ONE ABOUT PARENTAL INVOLVEMENT

 ## RELATED RESEARCH

A wealth of research highlights the positive link between parental involvement and a child's academic performance. Indeed, there is evidence to suggest that parental beliefs about their child's academic ability carries more weight in their child's mind than actual exam results (#39).

One such study (#9) found that having high academic expectations and regular communication were two of the most important parental behaviours and made the most impact on academic achievement. Parents should tread carefully, though, as it is not always a case of more being better. If expectations are excessively high, this can do more harm than good, as it increases stress and in the long term can reduce motivation.

The finding from this study that parental involvement was positively associated with teacher–student relationships is an interesting and important one, given that a lot of research highlights the numerous positive benefits for students and teachers to have a healthy dynamic. Therefore, anything that encourages this should be welcomed by all.

PARENTING IMPLICATIONS

The researchers of this study paint a clear picture when they say that parental "attitude is related to their child's academic performance". So how can parents use this finding practically on a day-to-day basis?

There doesn't appear to be one set way of doing this, since "longitudinal studies are needed to understand how these variables interact over time". Therefore, the findings from this study, whilst in sync with previous research, should be viewed with this perspective in mind. For now, offering warmth, support, high expectations and a good level of involvement is likely to offer the best route.

THE ONE ABOUT BAD DECISION-MAKING

@inner_drive | www.innerdrive.co.uk

THE STUDY

Why do students make decisions in the present that won't make them happy in the future? This dilemma is particularly pertinent for students who have to revise for exams that will have a significant impact on their lives. They know how important their exams will be, yet they don't always make good decisions in the present when it comes to preparation and revision. If we knew why this happened, then perhaps we would be better placed to help inform and guide students during these key periods of their education.

Fortunately, researchers specialising in thinking biases have investigated this for many years. Combining decades of research, psychologists from the University of Chicago have summarised why we make decisions and choose experiences that don't make us happy in the long run.

THE MAIN FINDINGS

People fail to make optimal decisions because *a)* they fail to predict future experiences accurately and *b)* they fail to follow through with their intentions.

1 Causes of failure to predict future experiences

Impact Bias

People **often over-estimate** the intensity and duration of positive events. This means **we think the highs will be higher** and last for longer.

Projection Bias

We **project our current feelings on to future events**, even when they are not relevant. As an example, the researchers state that "when people predict immediately after dinner how much they will enjoy a delicious breakfast the next morning, they understate the pleasure. They appear to reason as if because they are full now, they will also be full the next morning".

Memory Bias

When predicting future events, **we draw on how we felt about similar things** in the past. But past memories are fallible and are often susceptible to manipulation and riddled with inaccuracies.

2 Failure to follow through on intentions

Impulsivity

The **ability to delay gratification is hard**. Many would rather have less of a good thing now than more of the same thing in the long term.

Rule-Based Decisions

Sticking rigidly to rules or what one thinks one 'ought to do' or 'should do' **can lead to people being too rigid** and **not doing what is right for them** in that particular context.

Hsee and Hastie (2006). Trends in Cognitive Science.

THE ONE ABOUT BAD DECISION-MAKING

RELATED RESEARCH

This study neatly categorises two of the reasons that cause people to make poor decisions: we are bad at predicting the future and we are bad at following through with our intentions. In terms of being bad at predicting future behaviour, these findings align with previous research that found that we are not very good at guessing how long a task will take (#2). This is partially because we have a poor perception of time and suffer from a memory bias that over-values how we temporarily feel at the end of an experience or event (#76).

With regards to not following through on our intentions, evidence suggests that simply being motivated at the start of a task often isn't sufficient (#6). To convert intentions into behaviour change, it is important to delay gratification (#11, #26). By suffering a little in the short term, we can prosper more in the long term. Since we are highly drawn to instant rewards, this can be difficult, and there is evidence to suggest that some find it harder than others to delay gratification because of differences in their brains. Fortunately, other research has suggested ways to improve this; for example, if students trust the person giving them the instructions and if their environment is consistently reliable, it can help improve the ability to delay gratification.

PARENTING IMPLICATIONS

As students become older and progress through the education system, their ability to study independently becomes more important. These times of self-directed study, whether at home or during study periods, can have a big impact on their exams (and indeed their future lives). Therefore, any evidence that can help them to make better long-term choices is very much welcomed.

Helping children reflect on previous events and project how they might feel in the future based on different outcomes offers a good route to them becoming better independent learners. Likewise, removing short-term distractions, getting plenty of sleep (#24, #72) and effective goal setting can help develop their impulse control.

THE ONE ABOUT AGE AND SELF-CONCEPT

@inner_drive | www.innerdrive.co.uk

THE STUDY

How much impact does being born early or late in the school year, have on a child's performance? Previous research on primary-aged students suggests this impact may be quite significant. This is not surprising given that the oldest child in a year group can be as much as 20% older than the youngest at the beginning of primary school.

In terms of academic ability, the impact of this age gap reduces as students get older. But what effect does it have on students' self-belief in their academic abilities? Researchers recently tested this by monitoring the age, self-beliefs and university applications of over 10,000 15-year-old Australian students.

THE MAIN FINDINGS

1 Compared to their peers, **students who are older** within the school year **rate themselves higher** in:

✔ **Maths ability**

✔ **English ability**

✔ **Overall academic ability**

2 Controlling for actual academic achievement, **being one of the younger students in the year was a negative predictor** of going to University.

3 However, **if self-belief levels, which are malleable, are high,** then being young in the school year does not have any significant impact.

Ref: Parker et al. 2019. *Journal of Educational Psychology.*

THE ONE ABOUT AGE AND SELF-CONCEPT

 ## RELATED RESEARCH

The Relative Age Effect is a term used to describe how those born early in the academic year tend to perform to a higher level than those born later. One study found a relationship between the month a child was born in and their performance in a phonics test at 5-7 years old, with those being born at the start of the school year performing significantly better.

Indeed, evidence from the Education Datalab highlights how the Relative Age Effect is more pronounced in primary students than secondary ones. This is partly because, the younger a child is, the difference between being born at the start of the school year rather than the end is a higher percentage of his or her total age.

Research from outside of education suggests that this effect is more widespread than many may have thought. Recent work on this effect in sport, which combined the findings of 38 different studies spanning 23 years, 14 sports and 16 countries, found that for every two participants born in the last quarter of an annual age group, there were over three participants who were born in the first quarter. More specifically, the researchers discovered that the youngest within the year group were less likely to participate in both recreational and competitive sport from under the age of 14, play at a regional or national standard aged 15-18, or go on to become an elite athlete.

PARENTING IMPLICATIONS

The Relative Age Effect may have a slight self-fulfilling prophecy to it. Being born late in the year means that these students are physically, emotionally and cognitively behind their elder peers to start with. But if this leads to these children being viewed as either not as smart or having behavioural difficulties, then this label can stick to them. This in turn could lead to teachers and parents - and indeed themselves - viewing children through this lens whilst also believing that it is a permanent feature of their personality. Therefore, it is advisable when giving feedback to focus on the task, processes and self-regulation instead of on them as a person (#44).

THE ONE ABOUT SELF-REGULATED LEARNING

@inner_drive | www.innerdrive.co.uk

THE STUDY

Years and years of research in cognitive psychology has found that some revision strategies, such as retrieval practice and spacing, are far more effective than others, like cramming and simply re-reading notes.

This may be what past research tells us, but recently researchers wanted to find out: how likely are students to select the best strategies for themselves when revising? Also, what impact does their mindset have on these choices, along with their motivation to revise well, and ability to do so efficiently?

THE MAIN FINDINGS

1 The **most popular revision strategy** was to re-read information, with **75%** **of students** stating they did this lots.

2 **66%** of participants indicated that they **used a form of retrieval practice**; with **flashcards** (**40%**) and **self-testing** (**46%**) being the two most prominent.

3 Students were just as likely to **space out their revision** (**39%**) as they were to **cram their revision** (**36%**).

4 **61%** of students **reported that they study whatever topic or subject is due soonest**, with only **20% prioritising and studying** in the areas they are the weakest at. This suggests that students **tend to be motivated by deadlines** rather than by managing their revision.

5 Students with a growth mindset were **more likely to value the effective revision strategies**, such as retrieval practice, compared to less effective strategies, such as simply re-reading their notes.

6 Students with a growth mindset were also **more likely to be intrinsically motivated to do their revision**, and those with a fixed mindset were more likely to need extrinsic motivation.

Ref: Yan et al. 2014. Journal of Applied Research in Memory and Cognition.

THE ONE ABOUT SELF-REGULATED LEARNING

 ## RELATED RESEARCH

This study builds on previous research which has helped to rank which study strategies are the most effective (#1). The previous research had found that strategies like retrieval practice (#20), spacing (#4) and interleaving (#75) are better than simply re-reading notes. However, this study now allows us to compare the most effective strategies with the most popular ones. Doing so is of great interest and value, as it suggests that, unfortunately for many students, the most commonly used strategy is actually the least effective.

This study also builds on previous research done on the growth mindset (#5). To date, a lot of this research has focused on how students with a different mindset feel, with evidence suggesting that those with a growth mindset have higher self-esteem, effort levels and have more emotional stability with regards to their academic performance (#56). This study, as far as we are aware, is the first to link mindset with revision techniques.

PARENTING IMPLICATIONS

The researchers of this study summarise part of their findings by stating that "individuals who believe that intelligence can be increased through effort were more likely to value the pedagogical benefits of self-testing, to restudy and to be intrinsically motivated to learn". They do urge some caution when interpreting their findings as "the research we report is correlational", but that "it is likely that effective self-regulated learning requires both understanding of what learning strategies are effective and an appreciation that effort and difficulty are central to the process of learning, rather than a sign of failure to learn".

This suggests that parents can adopt a two-pronged approach to helping their students to study better. Firstly, they can educate their children on the different types of study strategies, highlighting both the strategies' benefits and how to effectively utilise them. Secondly, when parents help students attribute their success to internal causes such as effort and studying, children well develop their mindset towards intrinsic motivation, which is a more robust and reliable form of motivation in the long term.

THE ONE ABOUT COGNITIVE LOAD

@inner_drive | www.innerdrive.co.uk

THE STUDY

Cognitive Load Theory highlights how working memory is limited, and if it is overloaded, then the transfer of information from working memory to long-term memory is hindered. This has an effect on the amount that students learn.

Having to receive information from two or more sources can place a burden on working memory, as focus is being spread too thinly. This is known as the Split-Attention Effect. In order to investigate this, researchers tested to see if students who were presented with 'integrated' diagrams (i.e., information embedded within the diagram) performed better than those who were given 'conventional' diagrams with the additional information below it.

THE MAIN FINDINGS

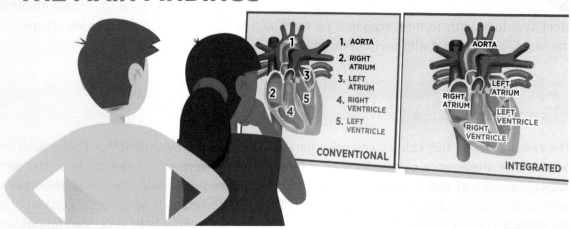

1 Students who were given information in an **integrated diagram took less time to process** the information than those who had to alternate between instructions and conventional diagrams.

2 Students who were given **integrated diagrams** also **performed better** on the exam, getting on average, **22%** higher marks.

Ref: Chandler and Sweller, 1992, British *Journal of Educational Psychology*.

THE ONE ABOUT COGNITIVE LOAD

 ## RELATED RESEARCH

This study is one of the seminal research papers that contributes to our understanding of Cognitive Load Theory. It builds on one of the most iconic psychological studies on working memory, which found that when participants were presented with a series of numbers one at a time on a screen, they could only accurately recall a sequence of 7 ± 2 items.

This current study has been referred to as the Split-Attention Effect, which forms a part of Cognitive Load Theory, as it highlights how asking students to split their attention between two sources simultaneously, causes cognitive overload (#35). Another part of Cognitive Load Theory is the Redundancy Effect, which is where giving students irrelevant information whilst they are learning something, clogs up their working memory. This means that students remember the wrong information, rather than the information you actually want them to remember. This is one of the reasons why revising whilst listening to music that has lyrics is not a good idea (#15).

PARENTING IMPLICATIONS

A child's working memory can be seriously impacted if they are receiving information from two or more places. Switching between different sources can lead to students remembering less content because their energy and resources are spent trying to process several things at the same time. This is why getting them to use integrated diagrams over traditional ones can be so helpful.

If a student is having to learn complex content (i.e., information that students have no previous experience with), then the more that students needs to split their attention, the more likely it is that cognitive overload will occur. If the material is easy to understand or has been encountered by students many times before, then students should gradually increase the complexity of the material.

Cognitive Load Theory is not without some challenges. It is notoriously hard (maybe impossible) to realistically measure cognitive load. It is also worth noting that Cognitive Load Theory talks about optimising load, not necessarily reducing it. The best way to think about it is through the Goldilocks Effect – the amount has to be just right. Too much cognitive load means that information will get lost, while too little cognitive load means that students just won't learn enough.

THE ONE ABOUT SCREEN TIME

@inner_drive | www.innerdrive.co.uk

THE STUDY

Students are growing up with an ever-increasing range of electronic devices at their disposal. This includes phones, TVs, computers and tablets. As such, it is an area of great concern for teachers and parents alike.

But what does the evidence say about the cost of screen time? It is not possible to say how much time spent in front of a screen is too much; however, a recent review of the existing research did highlight some very interesting findings.

THE MAIN FINDINGS

1 There is a **strong link** between **more screen time** and:

- ✔ **The likelihood of being obese**
- ✔ **Depressive symptoms**

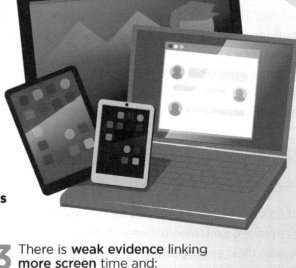

2 There is **moderate evidence** linking **more screen time** and:

- ✔ **Less healthy diets**
- ✔ **Eating high energy-dense foods**
- ✔ **Poorer quality of life**

3 There is **weak evidence** linking **more screen** time and:

- ✔ **Behavioural problems**
- ✔ **Anxiety**
- ✔ **Hyper-activeness and inattention**
- ✔ **Lower fitness levels**
- ✔ **Worse sleep**

4 The researchers also found that **small amounts of daily screen time** are not harmful and may have some benefits.

Ref: Stiglic and Viner, 2019, BMJ.

THE ONE ABOUT SCREEN TIME

 RELATED RESEARCH

A different study, of over 40,000 students between the ages of 2 to 17, found that greater hours of screen time were associated with lower well-being. Those students with a greater amount of screen time (7+ hours a day) often suffer from less curiosity, a lack of self-control and emotional instability. The same study found that even a moderate use of screens (4 hours a day) is associated with a lower psychological well-being.

Most of the research on the impact on screen time on adolescents has focused on televisions and less on computers and mobile phones. That being said, studies on the latter two technologies are emerging. For example, evidence suggests that excessive mobile phone use has a detrimental effect, partly because of how hard phones make it to focus on the task at hand (#25). Other research has noted the negative impact phones have on sleep if they are used up to two hours before bedtime (#34).

With regards to the findings that show a weak association between screen time and behavioural problems, anxiety, reduced fitness levels and sleep, the researchers do emphasise that "it is important to note that the weak evidence reported here largely relates to a lack of literature rather than weak associations". This suggests that more research is needed before we can draw firm conclusions.

PARENTING IMPLICATIONS

Enthusiasm for applying technology to learning runs the risk of going beyond what we currently know about the impact that it might have. It can clearly have some benefits, such as access to information and remote learning. However, it does have some drawbacks. For example, one study (#59) did find that students who take notes electronically typically do worse when they had to put this learning into practice (although this finding has not always been replicated).

Given the potential negative effects that this study associated with screen time, it is easy to see how students may be exposed to mixed messages if, on the one hand, they are taught that too much screen time is bad and on the other hand, they are encouraged to use the technology a lot for their schoolwork. Hopefully, more research can help guide us on how to walk this fine line.

THE ONE ABOUT PARENTS AND SLEEP

@inner_drive | www.innerdrive.co.uk

THE STUDY

The importance of regularly getting a good night's sleep shouldn't be underestimated. Decades of research have found it to be associated with better grades, attention, memory, mood, health and well-being. Yet despite this, many students aren't getting anywhere near the recommended amount.

Therefore, good sleeping habits are something that every parent should be thinking about for their child. But how accurate are parents at predicting how much sleep their child actually gets? To test this, researchers from Australia compared how much sleep 300 teenagers said they had had with how much their parents estimated they were getting.

THE MAIN FINDINGS

1 On a school night:

- Parents thought their child was going to bed **around 15-20 minutes earlier** each night than they actually were.

- Parents thought their child slept for almost **9 hours a night**, but students were getting much **nearer 8 hours**.

- Parents were pretty accurate at knowing **what time their child woke up in the morning.**

2 On the weekend:

- Parents thought their child was going to bed **between 20-30 minutes earlier** than they actually were.

- Parents thought their child slept for almost **10 hours a night**. In reality, they were actually getting **significantly less** than that.

- **Parents thought** their child was waking up later than they actually were – with some estimates being **almost an hour out**.

3 Overall, students **went to bed later, slept longer and woke up later** on the weekend compared to school days.

Ref: Short et al, 2013. *Nature and Science of Sleep.*

THE ONE ABOUT PARENTS AND SLEEP

RELATED RESEARCH

Other research has highlighted common sleep mistakes that students make. These include being on their phones or tablets too much (#34), going to bed at different times, napping for too long in the day, drinking high energy drinks late at night and over-thinking what they have to do tomorrow. Given the importance of sleep (#24), it is necessary to explore how we can encourage students to get more of it.

A recent study may have highlighted one way to do this. It investigated whether if older students were incentivised to get more sleep during exam periods, they would sleep more, and if so, would it lead to higher grades. The researchers offered extra credit for students who slept for at least 8 hours a night regularly (it should be noted that, for younger teenagers, this is still lower than the recommended amount). The researchers found that 71% of students who opted into the 8-hour deal got the required amount of sleep and higher marks than those who did not (even when the extra-credit marks were taken into account).

PARENTING IMPLICATIONS

The researchers note that "given many biopsychosocial factors which predispose adolescents to later sleep-onset time, plus the propensity for adolescents to access computers, mobile phones and music players after bedtime, parents may not be in a position to provide accurate estimates of sleep". This is important, since the evidence from this study shows "that adolescent sleep is likely to be much more restricted than their parents believe" but that they may be "unlikely to act if they are not aware that their teens are not obtaining sufficient sleep".

Therefore, it is vital to educate students about both the benefits of sleep and how to avoid common sleep mistakes. This can provide the platform and firm foundations to pro-actively cultivating a better and more beneficial night-time routine.

THE ONE ABOUT SUMMER LEARNING LOSS

@inner_drive | www.innerdrive.co.uk

THE STUDY

School summer holidays can be traced back to the Middle Ages; this was a time when there were many 'holy-days' and, with our agricultural history, many children were required to labour in the fields of their family farm during the summer months. But what impact do summer holidays have on a student's learning nowadays? And does it affect all students and all subjects equally? The seminal research, from over 20 years ago, which extensively reviewed the literature on this, makes for interesting reading.

THE MAIN FINDINGS

1 The Impact of the summer holidays:

▸ On average, **students regressed** by the equivalent of **one month** over the summer holidays.

▸ Students' **maths ability suffered the most** from summer learning loss. **Reading skills** are also negatively affected, but not by quite so much.

2 Who is affected by the summer learning loss?

▸ Evidence suggests that **middle class students do not suffer** from summer learning loss **as much as students from lower classes**.

▸ Summer learning **loss is not impacted** by a student's race or gender.

3 Why does summer learning loss occur differentially?

▸ The **range of activities that students are exposed to** during the summer holidays (e.g., It is easier to practice reading than it is to practice maths).

▸ The **way different types of knowledge decay over time**; "fact and procedure-based knowledge is more easily forgotten than conceptual knowledge".

Ref: Cooper et al, 1996, *Review of Educational Research.*

THE ONE ABOUT SUMMER LEARNING LOSS

 ## RELATED RESEARCH

The summer learning loss phenomenon makes sense given the wealth of evidence that has found the significant impact of student absenteeism on educational achievement. Research from the Department of Education recently found that every day missed by students was associated with a reduced chance of attaining 5 or more A*–C's at GCSEs. Given this, it is therefore unsurprising that there is such a cost to having six consecutive weeks off school.

Other research has explored deeper which students suffer the most during the summer. In support of this study's findings, researchers have found that students from lower socio-economic backgrounds feel the effects the most. Counter-intuitively, there is some evidence to suggest that students with an exceptional ability are also likely to significantly suffer.

Since this landmark study, subsequent research has focused on interventions to help reduce the decline in learning over the summer holidays. Two positive areas include summer schools and joint reading programmes that crucially engage both students and their parents.

PARENTING IMPLICATIONS

How can parents best help mitigate against the effects of summer learning loss? The researchers of this study note the different impact it has on different subjects and state that "the finding that subject area influenced the amount of summer loss may be due to the differential availability of opportunities to practice different academic material over the summer (with reading practice more available than math practice)". They therefore suggest setting students specific maths tasks to maintain their exposure to these sorts of subjects.

It is concerning to note that this study found that "the income differences also may be related to differences in opportunities to practice and learn (with books and reading opportunities more available to middle class students to use)". Of course, individual differences exist, and one should guard against making sweeping generalisations, but it is worth exploring free or assisted summer camps that can help reduce the negative impact that the summer holidays brings to overall learning.

THE ONE ABOUT KNOWING THE END IS NEAR

@inner_drive | www.innerdrive.co.uk

THE STUDY

Students have to work hard in order to do well in their exams and meet coursework deadlines. Some struggle with this as they can't see an end in sight. So, does knowing how much longer is left in the task help students to perform better during it? Surprisingly, this hasn't been researched much before.

To rectify this, researchers from the Tel Aviv University recently ran a study where, over two experiments, they had students complete a new, complex and boring learning task. They divided students into two groups: one group was updated on how much of the task was left and the other group wasn't.

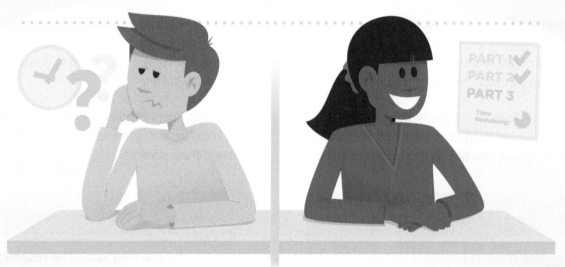

THE MAIN FINDINGS

The researchers found that if students knew how much of the task was left to do, compared to their peers who did not know, they:

1 Learnt at a **faster rate** and so achieved a **higher performance** quicker.

2 Felt **less fatigued** over the course of the task.

3 Took **shorter breaks** while completing the task – the researchers suggest that this was because "**knowing the end is near enhances motivation**". This was most pronounced towards the end of the tasks, where **those who were unaware** of how much time was left took breaks that were **up to twice as long** as those were aware.

Ref: Katzir et al, 2020. Cognition.

THE ONE ABOUT KNOWING THE END IS NEAR

RELATED RESEARCH

This study supports and adds an interesting new dimension to previous research on how hard students work to complete tasks, and how effectively they learn whilst completing them. Previous studies have found that many students tend to procrastinate, though their performance and efficiency is improved if they have deadlines to work towards (#47).

Part of this procrastination is due to students under-estimating how long a task will take to complete (#3). Providing feedback on how long is left in the task can help combat this. Research suggests that, once we know the end is near, people tend to accelerate their behaviour. As the authors of the study noted, "it has been found that the rate at which consumers buy coffee increases the closer to finishing a stamp card and receiving free coffee" and also that "runners increase speed closer to a finish line".

Another potential reason why the students in this study performed better if they knew how long was left in the task was that the fog of uncertainty was lifted. This freed students up to focus more on the task at hand. Other research has found a strong link between uncertainty and stress (#51). It appears that providing updates gives clarity which enhances both motivation and mood.

PARENTING IMPLICATIONS

Parents can apply the findings of this study very simply and effectively by breaking tasks down into smaller sections and reminding children of how long is left in the task. The authors suggest how the "effects of boredom, and perhaps even disengagement, can be countervailed using a simple procedure of providing individuals information on their distance from the finish line. In applied contexts (e.g., classrooms, work) mentioning to students how many more problems are left to solve or informing workers how close they are to end of a shift can have beneficial outcomes for performance as well as for affect and well-being".

THE ONE ABOUT INTERLEAVING AND DISCRIMINATION LEARNING

THE STUDY

@inner_drive | www.innerdrive.co.uk

Students often have to learn similar sounding yet very distinct concepts. For example, in biology, students have to learn about "transcription, transduction, transformation and translation – four terms with similar spellings and meanings." Students often struggle with this. Being able to distinguish between similar-sounding concepts is known as "discrimination learning".

Interleaving has been found to enhance learning and memory; it is the process of mixing up the order of topics that students learn so as to help them make connections and choose the best strategy when solving a different problem (the opposite being "blocking", which is covering one topic exclusively at a time). So, could interleaving help aid students to distinguish between their learning of similar concepts better? Researchers carried out a review of the existing literature to find out.

BLOCKING | TOPIC 1 | TOPIC 2 | TOPIC 3 | TOPIC 4

INTERLEAVING | TOPIC 1 TOPIC 2 TOPIC 3 TOPIC 4 | TOPIC 2 TOPIC 1 TOPIC 3 TOPIC 4 | TOPIC 3 TOPIC 4 TOPIC 1 TOPIC 2 | TOPIC 3 TOPIC 4 TOPIC 1 TOPIC 2

THE MAIN FINDINGS

Interleaving was found to:

1 Help students **improve their discrimination** learning. This is because with blocked practice "students need not identify an appropriate strategy because every problem in the assignment can be solved by the same strategy".

2 Help students **perform better** in final exams.

3 Work in a **range of subjects** – maths, art and sport were **specifically highlighted**.

4 Be **beneficial for a large age range of students** from primary through to university students.

Ref: Rohrer, 2012, Educational Psychology Review.

THE ONE ABOUT INTERLEAVING AND DISCRIMINATION LEARNING

RELATED RESEARCH

Research suggests that interleaving practice is effective in helping students to improve their learning (#1). This study helps to highlight the mechanism involved. Other studies support the long-term nature of this effect: in particular, one study found that when students were given a surprise test a month after learning the study material, those that interleaved their learning outscored the blocked group by almost double.

Not only is interleaving useful in academics, but the positive effects of it can also be seen in other fields, such as sport. For example, research shows that when PE students had to learn three different types of badminton serves, those in the interleaved group who practiced the serves in a random order, performed better later on than those in the blocked group.

PARENTING IMPLICATIONS

Interleaving is beneficial to students for many reasons, meaning that its popularity in education is justified. But as with any new and exciting concept, it can be misunderstood. This means that several interleaving myths exist. One such myth is that interleaving is the same as spacing (#4). Spacing concerns time, and it suggests that revisiting the same material often is more effective than studying in one chunk. Interleaving, on the other hand, is about mixing up the order of topics. This of course means that there is an element of spacing to interleaving, but not all spacing is interleaving.

Another misconception around interleaving is that it involves mixing up subjects as well as topics. Interleaving is effective as it helps students to make connections between related concepts and/or helps them to focus harder on choosing an appropriate strategy. This means that unrelated subjects may not get a benefit from interleaving.

The final misconception about interleaving is that it is a quick win. Research (#13) has found that if students were tested on the same day that they had learnt the material, their performance was much better if they had blocked their studying. However, when students were tested on their abilities one week later, performance in the interleaved condition was vastly superior. Given that many students are tested a month, a year, or two years after first being taught something, it suggests that parents would do well to encourage students to interleave their study and revision when at home.

THE ONE ABOUT THE PEAK END EFFECT

@inner_drive | www.innerdrive.co.uk

THE STUDY

Ever noticed how pop stars save their best song until last at a gig? This is because they want you to have the best time right at the end, so that you leave thinking the whole concert was great. This is an example of the Peak End Effect, in which people remember and place more weight on the end of an experience than on the experience as a whole.

This psychological quirk was first studied in the early 1990s by pioneering psychologist Daniel Kahneman and his colleagues in a fascinating study. The researchers subjected their participants to two unpleasant experiences. In part one, they had each individual place their hands in 14°C water for one minute. In part two, the participants had to again place their hand in 14°C water for one minute and then in 15°C water for an additional 30 seconds. After both of these experiences, the participants then had to choose which of the two experiences they wanted to repeat. Would they choose 60 seconds of a lot of unpleasantness, or 60 seconds of a lot of unpleasantness followed by 30 seconds of a bit of discomfort?

THE MAIN FINDINGS

1 **69%** of participants **chose to repeat the longer trial**. The researchers note that "this proportion would be zero if subjects acted to **minimize their exposure to pain**". Additional tests showed that "choices did not depend on whether the long trial was experienced first or second or with the dominant or nondominant hand".

2 The participants **who found the slightly warmer water** in the second trial much less unpleasant were **far more likely** to repeat the longer trial.

3 Most of the subjects stated that **the longer trial caused less overall discomfort**, was less tough to cope with and less cold at its most extreme moment.
But as the researchers reflected, "the long trial contained all the pain of the short trial and then some, these post-choice judgements are simply wrong". This means that participants chose to repeat the trial they **remembered as being easiest**, even if it wasn't. This is because they placed too much weight on the last 30 seconds of the trial.

Ref: Kahneman et al, 1993. Association for Psychological Science.

THE ONE ABOUT THE PEAK END EFFECT

RELATED RESEARCH

This seminal study helped changed the way psychologists (and indeed economists and many other professions) view human behaviour, as it has profound impacts on how we make decisions. In this case, by ending on a high – or, technically, not as bad a low – note, people remembered the event differently. This confirms that people have a subjective perception of both time and their experiences (#22). Other cognitive biases that since have been discovered include 'anchoring' (i.e., in which an initial number or piece of information weighs heavily in one's mind) and 'framing' (i.e., whether the options are presented in either a positive or negative light).

One study on anchoring found that people who were given 5 seconds to estimate the total of the calculation 1x2x3x4x5x6x7x8, guessed a much lower total (on average, 512) than those who were presented with the calculation written as 8x7x6x5x4x3x2x1 (average guess was 2,250). This is because, in the latter version, the numbers were higher at the beginning and as such were anchored in the participants' minds. (The correct answer is actually much higher than any of these guesses: 40,320.)

In a study into framing, people were asked to make medical decisions based on whether there was a 90% survival rate versus a 10% chance of dying. Despite representing the same probability, this led to very different decisions being made. Likewise, a different study into students found that 93% of them registered early for a course when a fine for being late was highlighted, yet only 63% did so if they were told they would receive a discount for registering early.

PARENTING IMPLICATIONS

This study can be used by parents, since it suggests that the last memory of an incident will have a big impact on how they felt about the experience as a whole. This can be useful when it comes to motivating bored students, dealing with times when they are likely to get distracted (#41) and improving the likelihood of them not forgetting key pieces of information (#55). Just as pop stars play their best songs to finish a concert, it would probably be a wise idea for parents to ensure their child finishes any given activity on a positive note, so that connection and feeling is embedded in their memory.

THE ONE ABOUT IMPORTANCE OF FAILING

@inner_drive | www.innerdrive.co.uk

THE STUDY

The researchers of this paper opened with the brilliant quote by Nobel prize winner Robert Lefkowitz, who said, "Science is 99 percent failure, and that's an optimistic view". So, as well as being somewhat inevitable, is failure also essential?

To test this, researchers from Universities in China and America recently tracked early-career scientists applying for national grants. They compared those who had failed to win a grant by a small margin (labelled "near misses") with those who had just obtained the required threshold (labelled "near wins").

THE MAIN FINDINGS

1 **10%** of these early career scientists who experienced a "near miss" **were highly demotivated** and this led to them not applying for research grants again.

2 Those who experienced a **"near miss" early in their career** had a similar number of research papers published over the **next 10 years** to those who had experienced a "near win" at the beginning of their career.

3 Fascinatingly, when looking at **who had published** a "hit" paper in the subsequent five years (which was defined as being in the top **5%** of cited papers), the "near miss" scientists, were over **20% more likely to have published a "hit" paper**, compared to the "near winners".

4 The researchers also found that the "near misses" were **more likely to have had their work cited by other scientists** and there was more potential to have their work translated into other languages. The researchers say these results show that the mantra of "what doesn't kill you **makes you stronger**" may indeed be true.

Ref: Wang et al, 2019. Nature Communications.

THE ONE ABOUT THE IMPORTANCE OF FAILING

 ## RELATED RESEARCH

The main finding that early failures may help budding scientists is an interesting one, given that separate research has indicated that if students hear about scientists who have failed at some stage in their career then they feel more connected to them. Subsequently, this led to students achieving higher grades in their science exams (with this impact being felt most strongly for students who had previously been struggling). One possible mechanism that causes this is the realisation that failure need not be fatal; this may help invoke and inspire a growth mindset, which has been shown to help resilience, self-esteem and enjoyment in the task itself (#5)

Previous research into the effect of success and failure has shown a large range of findings. Some studies have shown a Matthew Effect (i.e., the rich get richer) since early success can help fuel future successes because of enhanced recognition, confidence, motivation and resources. Other studies, however, have shown the potential benefits of failure, which include learning from the experience, boosted motivation, developing resilience and increasing compassion.

PARENTING IMPLICATIONS

The researchers flag a clear warning that, despite the powerful effect that early failure can have on the likelihood of one's future success, "one should not put roadblocks in the way of junior scientists, as the precondition of becoming stronger is not to be killed in the first place". Essentially, failure is a double-edged sword – it can both help and hinder – so it would be a mistake to artificially manufacture failure too much.

Instead, researchers suggest that their findings should be taken as a sign of comfort for those who do struggle, as "for those who persevere, early failure should not be taken as a negative signal – but rather the opposite", in line with Shinya Yamanaka's advice to young scientists, after he won the Nobel prize for the discovery of iPS cells, "I can see any failure as a chance".

Tips

Tips for improving memory

So what should your child do to improve the chances of making their learning stick? Evidence suggests that the following strategies offer the best bang for your buck:

✓ **Retrieval practice** – This is any activity that forces your child to come up with answers.

✓ **Space out learning** – Doing little and often is better than doing a lot all at once.

✓ **Interleaving** – Varying the type of problems they answer within a topic.

✓ **Elaborative interrogation** – Getting your child to ask "why is this the case?" or "why is this true for X but not for Y?".

✓ **Dual coding** – Combine pictures and words – this utilises dual coding, the production effect and reduces chances of cognitive overload.

✓ **Don't listen to music** – (Especially those with lyrics) when learning new or complex material. It really won't help.

✓ **Don't simply re-read the material or just highlight key passages** – These activities can be done on autopilot, which does not lead to deep and lasting learning.

✓ **Teach the material to someone else** – This helps them learn the material more deeply and organises their knowledge.

Tips for improving mindset, motivation and resilience

To help encourage a learning mindset and to prompt high levels of effort and persistence:

✔ **Help your child believe that they can improve and get better** – This can be done by focusing on:
- Effort and study strategies instead of natural ability
- Processes as well as the outcome
- Viewing mistakes as feedback and as an opportunity to learn

✔ **Developing a sense of purpose** – Help them connect their current activity with how it will help them achieve their future goals.

✔ **Explaining failures** – Encourage your child to not always internalise the causes of their failures, as this will reduce resilience.

✔ **Explaining successes** – Prompt them to reflect on their success. If they attribute it to external factors or luck, this will chip away at both their motivation and confidence.

✔ **Seek out support** – Encourage your child to use the support available to them. Help them see that asking for help is a sign of strength, not of weakness.

✔ **Control the controllables** – Remind them to focus on what is important and what is within their control.

✔ **Challenge and support** – For resilience to thrive, an environment must be both demanding and supportive.

✔ **Embrace failure** – This can help boost motivation, learning and resilience.

Tips for improving self-regulation and metacognition

Having high self-awareness and the ability to choose helpful thought processes and strategies is the bedrock of learning. This can be maximised by:

✓ **Getting plenty of sleep** – Teenagers and adolescents need it more than adults. Aim for 8–10 hours.

✓ **Controlling the inner narrative** – How your child talk to themselves will impact how they think, feel and behave.

✓ **Managing mobile phones** – Students who don't have them around concentrate more and learn more efficiently.

✓ **Improve self-reflection** – Encourage your child to ask themselves:

- Which resources will help me study?
- Why is this resource helpful?
- How will I use this resource?

✓ **Delayed gratification** – Sometimes it is better to suffer in the short term in order to prosper in the long term.

✓ **Distractions** – Students are more likely to be distracted on Mondays and Fridays; knowing this can help.

✓ **Don't say don't** – It is better for them to focus on what they do want and not on what they don't want.

✓ **Not all stress is bad** – Stress is often driven by uncertainty, but not all stress is bad. If children focus on how it will help them, then it will boost performance.

Tips for students

Actions speak louder than words. There is little point in students having good intentions if they don't convert them into positive behaviours. Here are some simple strategies that they can start implementing straight away that will lead to better learning:

- ✔ **Eat breakfast** – It is one of the easiest ways to boost mood, memory and grades.

- ✔ **Take notes during class** – To do this effectively:
  - Use pen and paper instead of laptops
  - Don't write everything down word for word; summarise it in their own words
  - Make notes at the end of each section or topic

- ✔ **Have high aspirations and expectations** of themselves whilst at school.

- ✔ **Choose study mates carefully** – Effort is contagious.

- ✔ **Turn down the backlight** on mobile phones a few hours before bed – it will help them sleep much better.

- ✔ **Don't spend too long daydreaming about the perfect future** – It can be distracting and lead to procrastination. If they do visualise things about the future, it is better for them to picture behaviour that will actually lead to their success.

- ✔ **Manage screen time** – Excessive screen time may make them think and feel worse.

Tips for parents

Parents want the best for their child. The following hit-list provides a strong foundation to support your child's learning and development:

✔ **Have high academic expectations for your children** – No-one rises to low expectations and research suggests that this is the most important thing parents can do to help boost their child's academic achievement.

✔ **Read with your children** and do so regularly from a young age.

✔ **Respond well to failures and mistakes** by taking time to discuss how these are learning moments. Your children will be more likely to develop a growth mindset.

✔ **Don't overpraise** – It conveys low expectations and if done in comparison to other children can lead to your child developing narcissistic behaviour.

✔ **When you praise, focus on their processes and behaviours,** instead of the outcome or their natural abilities.

✔ **Eat dinner together with your child regularly** when possible; it offers invaluable time together to discuss how school is going.

✔ **Have a clear structure and rules** around how your child divides their homework and leisure time. Taking the time to explain the thought process behind these rules will also help.

✔ **Be involved** - Parental involvement is positively associated with student achievement, student self-perception and teacher-student relationships.

✔ **Know how much they sleep** - Getting enough sleep is so important for developing adolescent minds.

Tips for overcoming thinking biases

We are all less rational and logical than we would like to think. The truth is, there are lots of thinking biases that get in the way of learning. To avoid some of the pitfalls, here is what you need to know:

✓ **You have less time to complete a task than you think** – So plan properly and start early.

✓ **Don't be seduced by natural talent** – We are poor predictors of what future talent may look like. Therefore, don't always fall for the allure of the present and try to imagine alternative future scenarios.

✓ **Better self-awareness** – We are more likely to criticise our past selves than our current one. This is a short-term self-protecting mechanism that can get in the way of accurately assessing our abilities and ideas.

✓ **Use objective data** – The lower our abilities are, the less accurately we are able to predict our current levels. Facts and stats are good ways to overcome this.

✓ **Don't fall for the spotlight effect** – People are often paying you far less attention than you think.

✓ **Don't fall in love with your own ideas** – We prefer our own ideas much more than those that someone else came up with. This makes it harder to take criticism or to know when to change approach.

✓ **Don't always follow the crowd** – This leads to people sometimes making bad decisions or doing things they wouldn't usually do.

✓ **Be a bit sceptical** – Don't fall for fancy explanations about learning styles. Always ask for the evidence.

✓ **Know how long is left in the task** – This can boost motivation, learning and effort.

✓ **Finish on a positive** – We tend to remember the last thing we experienced.

THE STUDIES

1 Dunlosky, J., Rawson, K. A., Marsh, E. J., Nathan, M. J., & Willingham, D. T. (2013). Improving students' learning with effective learning techniques: Promising directions from cognitive and educational psychology. *Psychological Science in the Public Interest, 14*(1), 4–58.

2 Khattab, N. (2015). Students' aspirations, expectations and school achievement: What really matters? *British Educational Research Journal, 41*(5), 731–748.

3 Buehler, R., Griffin, D., & Ross, M. (1994). Exploring the "planning fallacy": Why people underestimate their task completion times. *Journal of Personality and Social Psychology, 67*(3), 366.

4 Cepeda, N. J., Vul, E., Rohrer, D., Wixted, J. T., & Pashler, H. (2008). Spacing effects in learning a temporal ridgeline of optimal retention. *Psychological Science, 19*(11), 1095–1102.

5 Mueller, C. M., & Dweck, C. S. (1998). Praise for intelligence can undermine children's motivation and performance. *Journal of Personality and Social Psychology, 75*(1), 33.

6 Epley, N., & Dunning, D. (2000). Feeling "holier than thou": Are self-serving assessments produced by errors in self-or social prediction? *Journal of Personality and Social Psychology, 79*(6), 861.

7 Sebastian, C., Viding, E., Williams, K. D., & Blakemore, S. J. (2010). Social brain development and the affective consequences of ostracism in adolescence. *Brain and Cognition, 72*(1), 134–145.

8 Terman, L. M., & Oden, M. H. (1959). *The Gifted Group at Mid-life: Thirty-five Years Follow-up of a Superior Group.* Stanford, CA: Stanford University Press.

9 Castro, M., Expósito-Casas, E., López-Martín, E., Lizasoain, L., Navarro-Asencio, E., & Gaviria, J. L. (2015). Parental involvement on student academic achievement: A meta-analysis. *Educational Research Review, 14*, 33–46.

10 Holdsworth, S., Turner, M., & Scott-Young, C. M. (2017). . . . Not drowning, waving: Resilience and university: A student perspective. *Studies in Higher Education*, 1–17.

11 Shoda, Y., Mischel, W., & Peake, P. K. (1990). Predicting adolescent cognitive and self-regulatory competencies from preschool delay of gratification: Identifying diagnostic conditions. *Developmental Psychology, 26*(6), 978.

12 Paunesku, D., Walton, G. M., Romero, C., Smith, E. N., Yeager, D. S., & Dweck, C. S. (2015). Mind-set interventions are a scalable treatment for academic underachievement. *Psychological Science, 26*(6), 784–793.

13 Rohrer, D., & Taylor, K. (2007). The shuffling of mathematics problems improves learning. *Instructional Science, 35*, 481–498.

14 Haimovitz, K., & Dweck, C. (2016). What predicts children's fixed and growth mind-sets? Not their parents' view of intelligence but their parents' views of failure. *Psychological Science, 27*(6), 859–869.

15 Perham, N., & Currie, H. (2014). Does listening to preferred music improve reading comprehension performance? *Applied Cognitive Psychology, 28*(2), 279–284.

16 Kruger, J., & Dunning, D. (1999). Unskilled and unaware of it: How difficulties in recognizing one's own incompetence lead to inflated self-assessments. *Journal of Personality and Social Psychology, 77*(6), 1121.

17 Gunderson, E., Gripshover, S., Romero, C., Dweck, C., Goldin-Meadow, S., & Levine, S. (2013). Parental praise to 1–3 year-olds predicts children's motivation framework 5 years later on. *Child Development*, 1–16.

18 Desender, K., Beurms, S., & Van den Bussche, E. (2016). Is mental effort exertion contagious? *Psychonomic Bulletin & Review*, *23*(2), 624-631.

19 Tsay, C. J., & Banaji, M. R. (2011). Naturals and strivers: Preferences and beliefs about sources of achievement. *Journal of Experimental Social Psychology*, *47*(2), 460-465.

20 Roediger III, H. L., & Karpicke, J. D. (2006). Test-enhanced learning: Taking memory tests improves long-term retention. *Psychological Science*, *17*(3), 249-255.

21 Wegner, D., Schneider, D., Carter, S., & White, T. (1987). Paradoxical effects of though suppression. *Journal of Personality and Social Psychology*, *53*(1), 5-13.

22 Wilson, A., & Ross, M. (2001) From chump to champ: People's appraisals of their earlier and present selves. *Journal of Personality and Social Psychology*, *80*(4), 572-584.

23 Pressley, M., McDaniel, M. A., Turnure, J. E., Wood, E., & Ahmad, M. (1987). Generation and precision of elaboration: Effects on intentional and incidental learning. *Journal of Experimental Psychology: Learning, Memory, and Cognition*, *13*(2), 291.

24 Walker, M. P., & van Der Helm, E. (2009). Overnight therapy? The role of sleep in emotional brain processing. *Psychological Bulletin*, *135*(5), 731.

25 Thornton, B., Faires, A., Robbins, M., & Rollins, E. (2014). The mere presence of a cell phone may be distracting. *Social Psychology*, *45*(6), 479-488.

26 Kidd, C., Palmeri, H., & Aslin, R. N. (2013). Rational snacking: Young children's decision-making on the marshmallow task is moderated by beliefs about environmental reliability. *Cognition*, *126*(1), 109-114.

27 Peper, R. J., & Mayer, R. E. (1986). Generative effects of note-taking during science lectures. *Journal of Educational Psychology*, *78*(1), 34-38.

28 Vergauwe, J., Wille, B., Feys, M., De Fruyt, F., & Anseel, F. (2015). Fear of being exposed: The trait-relatedness of the impostor phenomenon and its relevance in the work context. *Journal of Business and Psychology*, *30*(3), 565-581.

29 Forrin, N., & MacLeod, C. (2018). This time it's personal: The memory benefit of hearing oneself. *Memory*, *26*(4), 574-579.

30 Wesnes, K. A., Pincock, C., Richardson, D., Helm, G., & Hails, S. (2003). Breakfast reduces declines in attention and memory over the morning in schoolchildren. *Appetite*, *41*(3), 329-331.

31 Martin, A. J., Colmar, S. H., Davey, L. A., & Marsh, H. W. (2010). Longitudinal modelling of academic buoyancy and motivation: Do the 5Cs hold up over time? *British Journal of Educational Psychology*, *80*(3), 473-496.

32 Gilovich, T., Medvec, V. H., & Savitsky, K. (2000). The spotlight effect in social judgment: An egocentric bias in estimates of the salience of one's own actions and appearance. *Journal of Personality and Social Psychology*, *78*(2), 211.

33 Fletcher, D., & Sarkar, M. (2016). Mental fortitude training: An evidence-based approach to developing psychological resilience for sustained success. *Journal of Sport Psychology in Action*, *7*(3), 135-157.

34 Wood, B., Rea, M. S., Plitnick, B., & Figueiro, M. G. (2013). Light level and duration of exposure determine the impact of self-luminous tablets on melatonin suppression. *Applied Ergonomics*, *44*(2), 237-240.

35 Mayer, R. E., & Anderson, R. B. (1991). Animations need narrations: An experimental test of a dual-coding hypothesis. *Journal of Educational Psychology*, *83*(4), 484-490.

36 Nestojko, J., Bui, D., Kornell, N., & Bjork, E. (2014). Expecting to teach enhances learning and organization of knowledge in free recall of text passages. *Memory & Cognition*, *42*(7), 1038-1048.

37 Atir, S., Rosenzweig, E., & Dunning, D. (2015). When knowledge knows no bounds self-perceived expertise predicts claims of impossible knowledge. *Psychological Science*, *26*(8), 1295-1303.

38 Norton, M., Mochon, D., & Ariely, D. (2011). The "IKEA effect": When labor leads to love. *Harvard Business School*, 1-33.

39 Parson, J., Adler, T., & Kaczala, C. (1982). Socialization of achievement attitudes and beliefs: Parental influences. *Child Development*, *53*(2), 310-321.

40 Reeve, J., Jang, H., Carrell, D., Jeon, S., & Barch, J. (2004). Enhancing students' engagement by increasing teachers' autonomy support. *Motivation and Emotion*, *28*(2), 147-169.

41 Wammes, J., Boucher, P., Seli, P., Cheyne, J., & Smilek, D. (2016). Mind wandering during lectures I: Changes in rates across an entire semester. *Scholarship of Teaching and Learning in Psychology*, *2*(1), 13-32.

42 Miller, C., & Krizan, Z. (2016). Walking facilitates positive affect (even when expecting the opposite). *Emotion*, *16*(5), 775-785.

43 Crum, A., Salovey, P., & Achor, S. (2013). Rethinking stress: The role of mindsets in determining the stress response. *Journal of Personality and Social Psychology*, *104*(4), 716-733.

44 Hattie, J., & Timperley, H. (2007). The power of feedback. *Review of Educational Research*, *77*(1), 81-112.

45 Kross, E., Bruehlman-Senecal, E., Park, J., Burson, A., Dougherty, A., Shablack, H., Bremner, R., Moser, J., & Ayduk, O. (2014). Self-talk as a regulatory mechanism: How you do it matters. *Journal of Personality and Social Psychology*, *106*(2), 304.

46 Senechal, M., & LeFevre, J. (2002). Parental involvement in the development of children's reading skill: A five-year longitudinal study. *Child Development, 73*(2), 445-460.

47 Ariely, D., & Wertenbroch, K. (2002). Procrastination, deadlines, and performance: Self-control by pre-commitment. *Psychological Science, 13*(3), 219-224.

48 Zhao, L., Heyman, G., Chen, L., & Lee, K. (2017). Telling young children they have a reputation for being smart promotes cheating. *Developmental Science, 21*(3), e12585.

49 Pekrun, R., Lichtenfeld, S., Marsh, H., Murayama, K., & Goetz, T. (2017). Achievement emotions and academic performance: Longitudinal models of reciprocal effects. *Child Development, 88*(5), 1653-1670.

50 Berman, M. G., Jonides, J., & Kaplan, S. (2008). The cognitive benefits of interacting with nature. *Psychological Science, 19*(12), 1207-1212.

51 De Berker, A., Rutledge, R., Mathys, C., Marshall, L., Cross, G., Dolan, R., & Bestman, S. (2016). Computations of uncertainty mediate acute stress responses in humans. *Nature Communications, 7*, 10996.

52 Chen, P., Chavez, O., Ong, D., & Gunderson, B. (2017). Strategic resource use for learning: A self-administered intervention that guides self-reflection on effective resource use enhances academic performance. *Psychological Science, 28*(6), 774-785.

53 Pham, L., & Taylor, S. (1999). From thought to action: Effects of process-versus outcome-based mental simulations on performance. *Personality and Social Psychology Bulletin, 25*(2), 250-260.

54 Brummelman, E., Thomaes, S., Nelemans, S., Orobio, B., Overbeek, G., & Bushman, B. (2015). Origins of narcissism in children. *PNAS, 112*(12), 3659-3662.

55 Murre, J. M., & Dros, J. (2015). Replication and analysis of Ebbinghaus' forgetting curve. *PLoS ONE, 10*(7), e0120644.

56 Robins, R., & Pals, J. (2002). Implicit self-theories in the academic domain: Implications for goal orientation, attributions, affect, and self-esteem change. *Self and Identity, 1*(4), 313-336.

57 Pashler, H., McDaniel, M., Rohrer, D., & Bjork, R. (2008). Learning styles concepts and evidence. *Psychological Science in the Public Interest, 9*(3), 105-119.

58 Fulker, J., Story, M., Mellin, A., Leffert, N., Neumark-Sztainer, D., & French, S. (2006). Family dinner meal frequency and adolescent development: Relationship with developmental assets and high-risk behaviours. *Journal of Adolescent Health, 39*(3), 337-345.

59 Mueller, P., & Oppenheimer, D. (2014). The pen is mightier than the keyboard: Advantages longhand over laptop note taking. *Psychological Science, 25*(6), 1159-1168.

60 Asch, S. E. (1951). Effects of group pressure upon the modification and distortion of judgments. In H. Guetzkow (Ed.), *Groups, Leadership and Men; Research in Human Relations* (pp. 177-190). Oxford, UK: Carnegie Press.

61 Smith, A. M., Floerke, V. A., & Thomas, A. K. (2016). Retrieval practice protects memory against acute stress. *Science, 354*(6315), 1046-1048.

62 Kardas, M., & O'Brien, E. (2018). Easier seen than done: Merely watching others perform can foster an illusion of skill acquisition. *Psychological Science, 29*(4), 521-536.

63 Vasilev, M. R., Kirkby, J. A., & Angele, B. (2018). Auditory distraction during reading: A bayesian meta-analysis of a continuing controversy. *Perspectives on Psychological Science, 13*(5), 567-597.

64 Borman, G. D., Rozek, C. S., Pyne, J., & Hanselman, P. (2019). Reappraising academic and social adversity improves middle school students' academic achievement, behavior, and well-being. *Proceedings of the National Academy of Sciences, 116*(33), 16286-16291.

65 Schmeck, A., Mayer, R. E., Opfermann, M., Pfeiffer, V., & Leutner, D. (2014). Drawing pictures during learning from scientific text: Testing the generative drawing effect and the prognostic drawing effect. *Contemporary Educational Psychology, 39*(4), 275-286.

66 Topor, D. R., Keane, S. P., Shelton, T. L., & Calkins, S. D. (2010). Parent involvement and student academic performance: A multiple mediational analysis. *Journal of Prevention & Intervention in the Community, 38*(3), 183-197.

67 Hsee, C. K., & Hastie, R. (2006). Decision and experience: Why don't we choose what makes us happy? *Trends in Cognitive Sciences, 10*(1), 31-37.

68 Parker, P. D., Marsh, H. W., Thoemmes, F., & Biddle, N. (2019). The negative year in school effect: Extending scope and strengthening causal claims. *Journal of Educational Psychology, 111*(1), 118-130.

69 Yan, V. X., Thai, K. P., & Bjork, R. A. (2014). Habits and beliefs that guide self-regulated learning: Do they vary with mindset? *Journal of Applied Research in Memory and Cognition, 3*(3), 140-152.

70 Chandler, P., & Sweller, J. (1992). The split-attention effect as a factor in the design of instruction. *British Journal of Educational Psychology, 62*(2), 233-246.

71 Stiglic, N., & Viner, R. M. (2019). Effects of screentime on the health and well-being of children and adolescents: A systematic review of reviews. *BMJ Open*, *9*(1), 1-15.

72 Short, M. A., Gradisar, M., Lack, L. C., Wright, H. R., & Chatburn, A. (2013). Estimating adolescent sleep patterns: Parent reports versus adolescent self-report surveys, sleep diaries, and actigraphy. *Nature and Science of Sleep*, *5*, 23-26.

73 Cooper, H., Nye, B., Charlton, K., Lindsay, J., & Greathouse, S. (1996). The effects of summer vacation on achievement test scores: A narrative and meta-analytic review. *Review of Educational Research*, *66*(3), 227-268.

74 Katzir, M., Emanuel, A., & Liberman, N. (2020). Cognitive performance is enhanced if one knows when the task will end. *Cognition*, *197*, 104189.

75 Rohrer, D. (2012). Interleaving helps students distinguish among similar concepts. *Educational Psychology Review*, *24*(3), 355-367.

76 Kahneman, D., Fredrickson, B. L., Schreiber, C. A., & Redelmeier, D. A. (1993). When more pain is preferred to less: Adding a better end. *Psychological Science*, *4*(6), 401-405.

77 Wang, Y., Jones, B. F., & Wang, D. (2019). Early-career setback and future career impact. *Nature Communications*, *10*(1), 1-10.